# GENEALOGICAL RESOURCES
### of the
### Minnesota Historical Society
## A GUIDE

# GENEALOGICAL RESOURCES
## of the
## Minnesota Historical Society
## A GUIDE

*Second Edition*

by the
Minnesota Historical Society
Library and Archives Division

MINNESOTA HISTORICAL SOCIETY PRESS
ST. PAUL

## ACKNOWLEDGEMENTS

The first and second editions of this guide were produced by the following staff members of the Minnesota Historical Society: Marcia Anderson, Ruth Bauer Anderson, Toni Anderson, Tracey Baker, James E. Fogerty, Lila Johnson Goff, Mark Greene, Patricia C. Harpole, Sue E. Holbert, Barbara M. Jones, Mary Klauda, Dallas R. Lindgren, Lydia Lucas, Dennis Meissner, Steven Nielsen, David Nystuen, Alan Ominsky, Wiley R. Pope, Ann Regan, Charles Rodgers, Alissa L. Rosenberg, Brigid F. Shields, F. Hampton Smith, Deborah Swanson, Duane Swanson, Jon Walstrom, John Wickre, and Bonnie Wilson. Nonstaff members Marilynn Taylor (copy editor) and Paula Stuart Warren, C.G.R.S. (reader), assisted with the first edition.

MINNESOTA HISTORICAL SOCIETY PRESS
St. Paul 55102

Manufactured in the United States of America
10 9 8 7 6 5 4 3 2 1
International Standard Book Number: 0-87351-240-5

♾ The paper used in this publication meets the minimum requirements of the American National Standard for Information Sciences — Permanence for Printed Library Materials, ANSI Z39.48-1984.

Library of Congress Cataloging-in-Publication Data
Minnesota Historical Society.
    Genealogical resources of the Minnesota Historical Society: a guide / by the Minnesota Historical Society, Library and Archives Division.
        p. cm.
    ISBN 0-87351-240-5 (alk. paper)
    1. Minnesota — Genealogy — Bibliography — Catalogs. 2. Minnesota Historical Society — Catalogs. I. Minnesota Historical Society. Division of Library and Archives. II. Title.
Z1299.M67 1989
[F605]
016.929'3776 — dc20                                        89-3305
                                                            CIP

*The illustrations used in this book are from the collections of the Minnesota Historical Society. The photograph on page 40 appears through the courtesy of the* St. Paul Dispatch.

# CONTENTS

# INTRODUCTION

In 1989 the Minnesota Historical Society (MHS) published the first edition of *Genealogical Resources of the Minnesota Historical Society: A Guide* to give researchers a sampling of its vast and varied resources. Since that time, many new items have been added to the collections, but more significant has been the gathering of all resources into one research facility in St. Paul, the state capital, made possible when the Society moved into Minnesota's new History Center in 1992.

This guide was compiled for at least two groups of researchers. For the numerous genealogists who have already used the resources of the MHS for documenting family and local history, it will point out stones left unturned. For other historians, the guide will identify resources for topics of the new social history—studies of gender, families, ethnic groups, the urban and rural pasts, material culture, labor, and "ordinary people." The holdings of the Society are huge and the quantity of materials for an individual resource can range from a few pages to thousands of boxes. The materials may be partial or complete; some continue to be added to and some cover a definite time span. This book, while ambitious, cannot be a complete inventory of all resources, but it can serve as a guide to many of them and introduce even the most experienced researchers to new areas for exploration.

Minnesotans typically leave records of births, marriages, and deaths, education, employment, religious and political affiliations, military service, property ownership, and relationships to governments and the law—all the way from paying taxes and registering a business to serving time in correctional facilities. The MHS has many of these records, as well as other items. The Society, founded in 1849 and the state's oldest institution, has long been recognized as the key repository for Minnesota's history. Besides holding collections of printed materials and the papers of prominent and not-so-prominent residents and businesses, the MHS is a designated legal repository for most of the state's newspapers and for the Minnesota State Archives.

The main feature of this guide is an alphabetical, annotated listing of resources by name of subject area. The entry for each resource describes content, location, and means of access. The use of computer catalogs, State Archives notebooks, Manuscripts Collections inventories, and supplemental card catalogs and finding aids enable the researcher to locate resources regardless of format. Any available index and any restrictions are noted. Special permission is required to obtain access to some restricted resources. Researchers wishing to use such resources should contact the MHS for any necessary instructions or forms before visiting. Many helpful publications that are mentioned in the resource entries are described more fully in Appendix 1, along with other items useful to researchers in Minnesota genealogy.

Current information about the location, hours, and telephone numbers of the Minnesota History Center is found in Appendix 2. Research services offered by the staff may be limited due to financial and time constraints.

Appendix 3 has general genealogical information about Minnesota, including addresses for vital records repositories, county courthouses, and historical and genealogical organizations.

With the publication of this book, the Minnesota Historical Society is pleased to provide a guide to a personal journey into the past for both beginning and experienced researchers who have discovered the value and pleasure of genealogy.

# GENEALOGICAL RESOURCES

- **ADOPTION RECORDS** *see* Court Records: Civil Case Files

- **AFRICAN AMERICANS: RESOURCES** *see* Ethnic Resources; Oral Histories; Appendix 1: Ethnic Sources

- **ALIEN REGISTRATION RECORDS**                    State Archives

  A February 1918 listing of all non-U.S. citizens in Minnesota, conducted by order of the Minnesota Commission of Public Safety. The two-page form includes information about a person's place and date of birth, port of entry and date of arrival in the United States, occupation, names and ages of children, and financial situation, as well as information about male relatives taking part in World War I.

  *Access:* State Archives notebooks: Public Safety Commission, Alien Registration. The records are arranged by county and then by city or township. A card index is available that lists individuals alphabetically by surname.

- **AMERICAN INDIANS: RESOURCES** *see also* Business Records: Fur Trade; Cemetery Records; Ethnic Resources; Land Records: Registers of Land Entries; Newspapers; Religious Records: Episcopal Church Records; Appendix 1: Ethnic Sources, Religious Sources

  The MHS collections are particularly rich in material about the two major Minnesota tribes—the Dakota (or Sioux) and the Ojibway (or Chippewa). In 1969 the Society published a bibliographic guide to some of its holdings as *Chippewa and Dakota Indians: A Subject Catalog of Books, Pamphlets, Periodical Articles, and Manuscripts in the Minnesota Historical Society* (see Appendix 1: Ethnic Sources). Much has been added to the MHS collections since then. Researchers should also consult the Sound and Visual Collections finding aids for holdings of more than 4,000 photographs of Minnesota Indian individuals, groups, and activities.

                    State Archives; Manuscripts Collections

  Microfilms of United States Bureau of Indian Affairs records, as well as allotment papers, Indian rolls, censuses, land records, subject files, treaty papers, curricula, correspondence, reports, legal materials, newspaper clippings, railroad records, and other papers from American Indians, government officials, lawyers, missionaries, clergy, and others.

  *Access:* State Archives notebooks: pertinent state and local agencies. Manuscripts Collections catalog: name of person, name of tribe, U.S. Office of Indian Affairs, and pertinent subject entries. Some of the microfilms are available through Interlibrary Loan.

# A

*Dakota Indian John Bluestone and descendants at Birch Coulee in 1903. Left to right (front row) are Maggie Wells, Andrew Good Thunder, Grace and Lillian Columbus, John ("Grandpa") Bluestone holding Alice Bluestone, Elizabeth, Henry, Betsy, and Agnes Wells, Tom, Mayme, and Delia Bluestone, (second row) Amos Wells, Lucy Wells Columbus, Willis Columbus, Charles and Emma Good Thunder, Mary Wells, James Bluestone, Frank Campbell, Clarence Lawrence, Lizzie and Hannah Wells, and (standing) Moses Wells, George Campbell, and Paul Lawrence holding Eliza Lawrence.*

Reference Collections

A comprehensive collection of published works about the Ojibway and the Dakota, with smaller collections about other tribes. Significant publications include items about wars, folklore, religion, social customs, biography, and government relations and treaties, as well as such multivolume works as United States Indian Office, *Report of the Commissioner of Indian Affairs* (1849–1923), and United States Department of the Interior, *Biographical and Historical Index of American Indians and Persons Involved in Indian Affairs* (8 vols.).

*Access:* Catalog: name of tribe.

### Chippewa and Sioux Annuity Rolls                Manuscripts Collections

Information about the Chippewa (1841–1907) and Sioux (1849–1935) Indians who were paid annuities by the United States government under treaties negotiated between the tribes and the government. The rolls may give name of head of family; head's mark; number of men, women, children, and total number in each family; and amount of annuity paid.

*Access:* Manuscripts Collections catalog: U.S. Office of Indian Affairs. The records are arranged by the name of the band (usually a village or an association of families under one leader). They are on microfilm and available through Interlibrary Loan.

### Indian Rights Association Papers                Manuscripts Collections

Microfilm of records (1864–1973) of a private, national organization dedicated to protecting the interests and general welfare of American Indians. The records include correspondence, letterpress books, minutes, annual reports, financial records, association pamphlets, and printed materials. Some of the record topics are the United States Bureau of Indian Affairs; the protection of Indian living conditions; education and health care; legal aid to Indian groups; and opposition to Home Rule. The papers contain a substantial amount of information about the Chippewa in northern Minnesota.

*Access:* Manuscripts Collections catalog: Indian Rights Association Papers.

• **AMERICANIZATION SURVEY CARDS: RAMSEY COUNTY**

State Archives

A 1918 survey of families in St. Paul with names of family members; ward, precinct, and block number; church; lodge; and newspapers taken. The information about each person over 16 years of age includes age, sex, country of birth, race or nationality, years in the United States, citizenship status, whether English is spoken or written, whether any other language is spoken or written, marital status, birthplaces of father and mother, where attending English classes, physical defects, and occupation. For each person under 16 the survey also includes information about last school and grade attended and education.

*Access:* State Archives notebooks: Public Safety Commission, Woman's Committee of Ramsey County, Americanization Survey Cards. The records are not indexed.

• **ARTISTS: RESOURCES**

Reference Collections

Clippings of articles about Minnesota artists. Two files are kept, one by the Curator of Art and one by the Reference Collections. The articles are from newspapers, periodicals, exhibit catalogs, and exhibit résumés

*Access:* Request files by artist's name from staff.

• **ASIAN AMERICANS: RESOURCES** *see* Ethnic Resources; Oral Histories

*The Alien Registration and Declaration of Holdings form of 1918 for Philipp Maser, a seventy-one-year-old native of Russia who had arrived in the United States in 1902*

- **ASSESSMENT RECORDS** *see* Tax and Assessment Records

- **ATLASES** *see* Geographical Resources

- **BIOGRAPHICAL RECORDS** *see also* Family Histories

**Biography Collection**                                    Manuscripts Collections

Brief information, arranged alphabetically by name, about more than 750 persons. Biographical and autobiographical sketches and notes, wedding and baptismal certificates, appointments, letters, reminiscences, school records, clippings, and memorial statements are included here when the MHS does not hold an appropriate collection of personal or family papers.
*Access:* Manuscripts Collections catalog: name of person.

**Biography Files**                                           Reference Collections

Obituary citations and biographical sketches of Minnesotans in an alphabetical file. Begun in 1917, this file contains the names of about 100,000 persons, including farmers, doctors, educators, civic leaders, politicians, pioneer settlers, criminals, business executives, artists, actors, musicians, fashion designers, and authors. The references to persons are from newspapers, periodicals, and books within the Society's collections. The Minnesota Biographies Project (begun in 1976) has added another 50,000 names updating and enhancing the published volume of MHS *Collections* entitled "Minnesota Biographies, 1655–1912" (see Appendix 1: Minnesota Historical Sources).

The Reference Collections also has vertical files of miscellaneous newspaper clippings that contain biographical information and may be located under the individual's name in the category "Biography" or under subject categories such as "Authors," "Artists," "Aviation-Biography," "Musicians," or "Sports-Biography."
*Access:* Ask staff for assistance.

**Biography Reference Sets**                                  Reference Collections

*The American Biographical-Genealogical Index* (published 1952–   ; 169 vols.) indexes every name in about 800 publications of family and local history and in the 1790 United States census. The Reference Collections has almost 95 percent of the titles included in this index. Other significant publications include:

> *Dictionary of National Biography* (of Great Britain for persons deceased by 1921; 69 vols.)
> *Dictionary of American Biography* (of the United States for persons deceased by 1965; 20 original vols. reprinted in 10 vols.; 7 suppls.)
> *Who's Who in America* (published 1899/1900–   )
> *Who Was Who in America* (covering 1607–1976; 7 vols.)
> *American Ancestry: Giving the Name and Descent, in the Male Line, of Americans Whose Ancestors Settled in the United States previous to the Declaration of Independence, A.D. 1776* (1968; 12 vols.)
> *Appletons' Cyclopaedia of American Biography* (1887–89; 6 vols., with vols. 7–11 published 1900–28 as supplementary editions)
> *Lamb's Biographical Dictionary of the United States* (published 1900–1903; 7 vols.)

*Genealogical Index of the Newberry Library, Chicago* (published 1960; 4 vols.)

*Dictionary of Canadian Biography* (for persons possibly deceased by 1890; 11 vols. published, more in progress)

Lareau, Paul J., and Elmer Courteau, comps. *French-Canadian Families of the North Central States: A Genealogical Dictionary* (published 1980–81; 11 vols.)

Tanguay, Cyprien. *Dictionnaire Généalogique des Familles Canadiennes* (published 1871–90 in 7 vols.; 3 complements by J.-Arthur Leboeuf, published 1957–64)

*Répertoire des Actes de Baptême, Mariage, Sépulture, et des Recensements du Québec Ancien* (published 1980–90 in 47 vols.; more in progress).

For an every-name index to a variety of Minnesota-related genealogical, biographical, and historical sources, see Pope, comp., *Minnesota Genealogical Index*, vol. 1 (Appendix 1: Genealogical Sources).

*Access:* Catalog.

## B

- **BIRTH RECORDS** *see* Appendix 3: Vital Records Repositories

- **BLACK AMERICANS: RESOURCES** *see* Ethnic Resources; Oral Histories; Appendix 1: Ethnic Sources

- **BOND AND OATH RECORDS**                                State Archives

Elected and appointed officials of state and local governments post bonds and swear oaths to ensure that they will carry out the responsibilities of their offices. The records usually include name of officer, office to which elected or appointed, effective date and term of appointment, and name of bondholder. The records of the Territorial Secretary include oaths and bonds for territorial and local offices, 1849–57. The records of the Secretary of State, beginning in 1858, include oaths and bonds of elected state officials, appointees to statewide official posts, appointees to boards and commissions, and appointees to such offices as game warden and state inspector; they also contain registers of oaths and bonds of county officials, 1875–1914. Oaths and bonds of local officials (including officers of counties, cities, villages, townships, and school districts) are found in the records of the respective district court, County Auditor, and County Register of Deeds (Recorder). The statutes governing filing requirements for officeholders have varied significantly over time.

*Access:* State Archives notebooks: Territorial Records, Territorial Secretary; Secretary of State, Bonds and Oaths; county name, District Court; county name, Auditor; and county name, Register of Deeds. These records may be titled differently from county to county; occasionally, they are listed within the respective district court records. Some records are indexed.

- **BURIAL RECORDS** *see* Cemetery Records

- **BUSINESS RECORDS**

### Annual Reports                                Reference Collections

Available for many Minnesota businesses, annual reports typically include information about a company's progress, programs, activities, expenditures, and assets, and a statement of purpose. Some biographical information about officials or persons receiving awards may be included. Lists of employees are rarely attached to annual reports.

*Access:* Catalog: name of business.

### Business Histories                                    Reference Collections

Often published in commemoration of a milestone anniversary, the history of a business may include biographies of its founders, presidents, and members of its board of directors.

*Access:* Catalog: name of business. Some histories are individually indexed.

### Business Name Registrations                                State Archives

Registrations of all businesses unincorporated and doing business under a name other than the owner's, 1911–78. The registration includes certificate number, business name, business address, owner(s)'s name(s), and date of filing. Registration authority was transferred from County Clerks of Court to the Secretary of State on July 31, 1979.

*Access:* State Archives notebooks: county name, District Court. Registrations are not indexed.

### Company Newsletters                                Manuscripts Collections

Newsletters produced by publicity and personnel departments and employee organizations. These may contain information about individual employees, as well as retirements, mergers, awards, moves, investigations, and company policies.

*Access:* Manuscripts Collections catalog: name of company. Northern Pacific Railway Company notebooks: Advertising and Publicity. Great Northern Railway Company notebooks: Advertising and Publicity.

*Interior of the Addison Bros. Store in Marshall, about 1915*

Locating or identifying newsletters may be difficult because their titles do not always include the name of the company; examples are the *Modern Millwheel* (General Mills) and the *Northliner* (North Central Airlines).
*Access:* Catalog: name of company.

### Fur Trade Records                                    Manuscripts Collections

Daybooks, journals, ledgers, invoice books, business contracts, traders' accounts, diaries, correspondence, personal narratives, cargo manifests, and notary contracts. The records cover the North American fur trade from 1700 to the present and contain information about contracts between companies and individual traders, trading licenses, migration patterns, early settlements, and fur trade company and American Indian interactions. For information about early fur-trade manuscript sources in the collections of the MHS and elsewhere, see Bruce White, comp., *Fur Trade in Minnesota* (Appendix 1: Minnesota Historical Sources).
*Access:* Manuscripts Collections catalog: name of company; name of person.

### Incorporation Records                                        State Archives

Secretary of State records relating to the incorporation of for-profit and not-for-profit firms, 1858–1935. In addition to the main series of incorporations, several special series cover incorporations and amendments for Roman Catholic churches (1877–1912), religious corporations (1885–1929), state banks (1907–51), cooperatives (1919–28), and nonprofit firms (1946–52). The filings provide information about business names, purpose of the firm, dates of filing, amount of stock, and names and residences of incorporators. Additional records of incorporation of cooperatives (1927–70) are found in Minnesota Department of Agriculture Cooperatives Division materials.
*Access:* State Archives notebooks: Secretary of State, Corporation Division; Agriculture Department, Cooperatives Division. Two microfilm series of indexes (both alphabetical by name of corporation) cover the 1850s to 1986 and refer researchers to original incorporation records, in the State Archives, of Minnesota organizations established 1858–1935 and to original or microfilm records in the Secretary of State's office. The indexes are in two series: Active (in 1986) and Inactive (by 1986) Domestic Corporation Card Files. These indexes are *not* available through Interlibrary Loan. A fuller description of the correlations between records and indexes in the Secretary of State's office and in the State Archives can be found in the Secretary of State notebook. Ask staff for assistance.

### Makers, Manufacturers, and Businesses File        Museum Collections

Card file of Minnesota businesses and entrepreneurs, arranged by name and based on information drawn from letterheads, advertisements, newspapers, city directories, artifacts, and other sources.
*Access:* Ask staff for assistance.

### Textile Labels File                                      Museum Collections

Card file of Minnesota businesses, manufacturers, and persons related to the clothing industry, arranged by name on garment label. Because it includes dressmakers and milliners, the file is a good source for women's names.
*Access:* Ask staff for assistance.

**B**

Manuscripts Collections

The MHS holds unpublished collections of more than 600 businesses ranging in size from small grocery stores to multinational corporations. Payroll records and time books may list employee, employee number, job title, rate of pay, and hours worked. Annual reports, company newsletters, and employee newsletters also may contain information about individual employees.

*Access:* Manuscripts Collections catalog: name of company. Access to some records may be restricted.

# B-C

• **CEMETERY RECORDS** *see also* Correctional Facilities Records; Hospital Records; Newspapers

State Archives

Of interest to genealogists are burial records, cemetery plats, indexes to burials in hospital cemeteries, municipally owned cemeteries, obituary records, and listings of burials from Minnesota's state hospitals. Notable groups include Faribault State School and Hospital, Willmar State Hospital, Hastings State Hospital, Cambridge State Hospital, and St. Peter State Hospital. Minnesota Department of Health records include an incomplete 1933 statewide cemetery inventory listing the location and name of the cemetery and the name and address of the secretary or person in charge.

*Access:* State Archives notebooks: individual hospital names; Health Department, cemetery inventory; county, municipality.

Manuscripts Collections

Records of Minnesota cemeteries, cemetery associations, plats, lot records, burial records, certificates, gravestone inscriptions, and epitaphs. In the late 1930s the Historical Records Survey of the Work Projects Administration

*Bohemian National Cemetery, McLeod County, May 1912*

(WPA) conducted a survey that has information about many Minnesota cemeteries, including private and Indian burials and abandoned cemeteries. The survey form includes name of cemetery; county; township, village, or city; location; ownership; date established; date of first burial; dedication date; condition and history of cemetery; location of records; and source of information. The forms, which are arranged by county, do *not* list persons buried in the cemeteries.

*Access:* Manuscripts Collections catalog: name of cemetery; Work Projects Administration.

Reference Collections

Inscriptions copied from gravestones in cemeteries located in about half of Minnesota's counties. Complete lists for some counties have been published. Some inscriptions from practically all counties have been copied and published.

Many inscriptions have been published in periodical articles and are not listed separately in the Reference Collections catalog. Most of these articles are noted in *Minnesota Cemeteries in Print*, compiled and edited by Pope (see Appendix 1: Genealogical Sources), which includes out-of-state burials, statewide listings, and listings by county, subdivided by city or township. For help in locating a cemetery, see Pope and Fee, *Minnesota Cemetery Locations* (Appendix 1: Genealogical Sources), which identifies the locations of about 4,400 Minnesota cemeteries by county and approximate legal description of the land.

*Access:* Catalog: Cemeteries.

## • CENSUS RECORDS State Archives; Reference Collections

The earliest census listings for the area that later became Minnesota are found in the 1820 Michigan territorial census. The 1830 territorial censuses do not seem to include Minnesota. The 1836 Wisconsin territorial census, however, includes portions of present-day Minnesota as part of Crawford County and as part of Dubuque County (later in Iowa Territory). Portions of Minnesota are also in the 1838 Wisconsin Territory census as part of Crawford and Clayton counties. Minnesota inhabitants are included in the 1840 Wisconsin and Iowa territorial censuses.

Minnesota became a territory in 1849. Territorial censuses were conducted in 1849, 1850, 1853, 1855, and 1857. Complete sets of the 1853 and 1855 censuses do not survive, but listings for some communities in some counties are in the State Archives.

Minnesota achieved statehood in 1858. Two series of censuses were conducted after this time: one by the federal government (decennial years) and another by the state government (1865, 1875, 1885, 1895, and 1905). Additional censuses (nonpopulation schedules) for 1850, 1860, 1870, and 1880 gathered information about deaths, farms, industry, and communities.

There are microfilm copies of most of the above censuses in both the State Archives and the Reference Collections. Duplicates of some census schedules for occasional counties or townships for some years exist in the State Archives. These may contain more legible or more complete entries than those on microfilm.

| Families numbered. | | Name of every person whose residence was in this family on the 1st of May, 1875. | Age. | Sex. | Color. | Nativity, State or Country. | PARENT NATIVITY. | |
|---|---|---|---|---|---|---|---|---|
| | | | | | | | Father. | Mother. |
| 1 | 1 | *Levi's Johnson* | 44 | m | w | Norway | Nor. | Nor. |
| 2 | | *Anna T Johnson* | 54 | f | " | " | " | " |
| 3 | 2 | *C. P. Ingalls* | 39 | m | " | N.Y. | Can | N.Y. |
| 4 | | *Caroline Ingalls* | 35 | f | " | Wis. | Mass. | Mass. |
| 5 | | *Mary C. P. Ingalls* | 10 | " | " | " | N.Y. | Wis. |
| 6 | | *Laura C. Ingalls* | 7 | " | " | " | " | " |
| 7 | | *Carrie C Ingalls* | 5 | " | " | Kan. | " | " |
| 8 | 3 | *G. S. Thompson* | 32 | m | " | Can. | Scotland | Scotland |

*The 1875 Minnesota state census for Redwood County includes the Ingalls family: Charles and Caroline (who was 35 years old) and their daughters, Mary, Carrie, and Laura, who as Laura Ingalls Wilder later wrote the famous Little House books. On the Banks of Plum Creek is based on the family's experiences of living in a river-bank dugout in southwestern Minnesota at the time of the great grasshopper plague.*

**Access:** Microfilm copies of the 1820, 1840, 1850, 1857, 1860, 1865, 1870, 1875, 1880, 1885, 1890 Veterans', 1895, 1900, 1905, 1910, and 1920 Minnesota censuses as well as published copies of the 1849 and 1850 Minnesota censuses are available in the State Archives and the Reference Collections. Microfilm copies of the 1836 and 1838 Wisconsin censuses and the 1860, 1870, and 1880 Minnesota nonpopulation censuses are available. For other censuses, see State Archives notebooks: Census Records; Territorial Records; County name. Some Minnesota censuses are indexed—see the individual descriptions below. For information about obtaining census microfilms through Interlibrary Loan or purchase, see Appendix 2: Services.

### Population Censuses for Minnesota

*1849* Name of head of household; number of males; number of females. Published in Minnesota (Territory), Legislative Assembly, *Journal of the House of Representatives, First Session of the Territory of Minnesota,* 1850, Appendixes C and D, p. 195–215 (in Reference Collections).

*1850* Name; age; sex; color; occupation; value of real estate; birthplace (state or country); married within year; attended school within year; illiterate. Census and surname index published in Harpole and Nagle, eds., *Minnesota Territorial Census, 1850* (see Appendix 1: Minnesota Historical Sources).

*1853* (Incomplete.) Name of head of household; number of children; number in household; names of inhabitants (for some communities only).

*1855* (Incomplete.) Name of head of household; number of males; number of females; total number in household.

*1857* Name; age; sex; color; birthplace; voting status of male (native or naturalized); occupation of each male over the age of 15. Microfilm index by surname.

*1860* Same information categories as 1850, plus value of personal estate; deaf, dumb, blind, insane, pauper, convict. Microfilm and published indexes by surname; see Meissner, *Guide to the Use of the 1860 Minnesota Population Census Schedules and Index* (Appendix 1: Minnesota Historical Sources).

*1865* Name; sex; color; deaf, dumb, blind, insane; soldier in service on June 1, 1865.

*1870* Same information categories as 1860, plus census notes if father and mother of foreign birth; month of birth or marriage if occurred within last year; male citizen of United States age 21 and over; male citizen whose right to vote is denied. Microfilm index by county; within county by surname. Published index by surname gives page numbers for family entry and for agricultural entry.

*1875* Name; age; sex; color; birthplace (state or country); birthplaces of father and mother.

*1880* Same information categories as 1870, plus name of street; house number; relation of each person to head of household; marital status; number of months unemployed in previous year; whether ill or injured on day of enumeration; birthplaces of father and mother (state or country). Microfilm Soundex index (arranged phonetically by surname) lists only households with children under age of 10.

*1885* Same information categories as 1875, but instead of parents' birthplaces, census notes if father and mother are of foreign birth; plus deaf, dumb, blind, insane; soldier in Civil War.

*1890* Most of the United States population census was destroyed by fire in the 1920s. For Minnesota, one page for Rockford Township, Wright County, survived (*access:* on roll 3 of the 1890 census microfilm). The local copy for Rockville Township, Stearns County, also survived (*access:* State Archives notebooks: Census Records, Stearns County).

*1890* Veterans' Census. Name of surviving veteran or widow; rank; company; regiment or vessel; date of enlistment; date of discharge; length of service; post office address; disability incurred; and remarks. Incomplete published index by surname.

*1895* Same information categories as 1885, plus length of residence in state and enumeration district (years and months) of males; occupation; months regularly employed in previous year; if previously enumerated in census; omits deaf, dumb, blind, insane.

*1900* Same information categories as 1880, plus month and year of birth; mother of how many children and number of children living; year of immigration to United States; number of years in U.S.; naturalization; literacy; English speaking; ownership of home. Microfilm Soundex index (arranged phonetically by surname) lists all households.

*1905* Same information categories as 1895, plus street address; birthplaces of father and mother (state or country); length of residence for each person; service in Civil and Spanish-American wars.

*1910* Same information categories as 1900, plus length of marriage; language spoken; type of industry employed in; if employer, employee, or self-employed; number of weeks unemployed in 1909; if unemployed on April 15, 1910; if a survivor of the Union or Confederate armies or navies. Not indexed.

*1920* Name; address; relationship to family head; sex; race; age; marital status; if foreign born, year of immigration to the U.S.; whether natural-

C

ized, and year of naturalization; school attendance; literacy; birthplace of person and parents; mother tongue of foreign born; ability to speak English; occupation, industry, and class of worker; home owned or rented; if owned, whether mortgaged; for nonfarm mortgaged, market value, original amount of mortgage, balance due, interest rate. Microfilm Soundex (arranged phonetically by surname) includes all households.

*Access:* See above.

## Nonpopulation Censuses for Minnesota

Each census is for the 12 months preceding June 1 of the census year.

### Agricultural Censuses

*1850* Name of owner, agent, or manager of farm; acres of land; cash value of farm; value of farming implements and machinery; number of livestock; produce during year; value of animals slaughtered.

*1860* Same information categories as 1850.

*1870* Same information categories as 1850, plus amount of wages paid; estimated value of all farm production.

*1880* Same information categories as 1870, plus cost of fences; cost of fertilizer; weeks of hired labor; poultry; forest products.

### Manufacturing Censuses

*1850* Name of corporation, company, or individual; name of business; capital invested; raw materials used; kind of motive power and machinery; average number of employees; wages; annual products and value.

*1860* Same information categories as 1850.

*1870* Same information categories as 1850, plus number of months in active operation; materials and value.

*1880* Same information categories as 1870, plus greatest number of persons employed at one time.

### Mortality Censuses

*1850* Name of person who died in preceding year; age; sex; color; free or slave; married or widowed; place of birth; month died; occupation; cause of death; number of days ill.

*1860* Same information categories as 1850.

*1870* Same information categories as 1850 plus if father and mother of foreign birth; omits free or slave and number of days ill.

*1880* Same information categories as 1870 plus marital status; birthplaces of father and mother (state or country); length of residence in county; place where taken ill if other county; name of attending physician.

### Social Statistics Censuses

*1850* Lists by community the value of real and personal estate; annual taxes; crops; number and type of schools, libraries, newspapers, periodicals, and churches; pauperism; crime; wages.

*1860* Same information categories as 1850.

*1870* Same information categories as 1850, plus amount of public debt.

*1880* Provides information about homeless children; prisoners; paupers and indigents; deaf-mutes; blind; insane; idiots.

*Access:* See above.

In addition to the Minnesota federal and state censuses, the Reference Collections holds for other states a miscellaneous collection of published censuses and indexes, as well as microfilms. Full runs of censuses include, for example, complete 1790 United States census; 1830 Michigan Territory census; 1836, 1850, and 1860 Wisconsin territorial and state censuses; 1840 and 1860 Iowa territorial and state censuses; 1860, 1870, and 1880 Dakota Territory census; 1885 Dakota Territory census for the area that became North Dakota in 1889. *Access:* Card index of holdings.

C

• **CENTURY FARM APPLICATIONS** State Archives

Applications to the State Agricultural Society from residents who wished to have their farms designated century farms. The designation signified that the farm had been in the same family for 100 or more years. This was a joint project begun in 1976 by the Minnesota State Fair and the *Farmer* magazine. The forms give biographical and genealogical information and ownership history of the farm, and some include reminiscences.
*Access:* State Archives notebooks: Agricultural Society, Century Farm Application Forms. The forms are filed first by year, then alphabetically by county.

• **CHILD WELFARE SURVEY CARDS: RAMSEY COUNTY** State Archives

An incomplete 1918 survey giving name, address, sex, place of birth, whether birth was registered, age, height, weight, pounds underweight, serious disease or defect, name of examiner, and notes on follow-up contacts. The survey is for Ramsey County only.
*Access:* State Archives notebooks: Public Safety Commission, Woman's Committee of Ramsey County, Child Welfare Survey Cards. The survey is arranged by wards within the city of St. Paul.

• **CHIPPEWA INDIANS: RESOURCES** *see* American Indians: Resources

• **CHURCH HISTORIES** *see* Oral Histories; Religious Records

• **CORONERS' RECORDS** State Archives

Records of some County Coroners' offices giving name of deceased person, conclusion as to cause of death, name of Coroner, and other relevant information; may also contain records of an inquest.
*Access:* State Archives notebooks: county name, Coroner. Some records are indexed. Access to some information may be restricted.

• **CORONERS' REPORTS** State Archives

Certificates and records filed by the County Coroner in the district court. The information is similar to that in the Coroners' Records.
*Access:* State Archives notebooks: county name, District Court, Coroners' Records. Some reports are indexed. Access to some information may be restricted.

• **CORPSE PERMITS** State Archives

Record of permits (1898–1912) issued for the transportation of corpses, primarily to other states, although there were some intrastate shipments. Each register entry lists number and date of permit, name of deceased, date and

*Shingobe, his wife, and their daughter, Susan Sam Razor, had a family portrait made in Onamia, about 1909–12. The beadwork on Shingobe's clothing and bandolier (or shoulder) bag features traditional Ojibway floral designs.*

C

cause of death, destination, name of medical attendant, name of health officer, name of undertaker, name of escort, and railroad company transporting corpse.

*Access:* State Archives notebooks; Health Department, record of corpse permits. The permits are not indexed.

• **CORRECTIONAL FACILITIES RECORDS** *see also* County Records; Municipal Records; Newspapers

State Archives

Records of the Minnesota State Prison (Stillwater; 1851–  ), St. Cloud State Reformatory for Men (1887–  ), Red Wing State Training School for Boys (1866–  ), Sauk Centre Home School for Girls (1911–  ), Shakopee State Reformatory for Women (1920–  ), and St. Peter Security Hospital (1907–  ), and some from the Forestry Camp at Willow River (1951–  ). Records vary from facility to facility, but may include inmate case files, admission and discharge registers, commitment papers, parole records, school records, inmate photographs, population reports, trial transcripts, hospital or clinic records, and disciplinary records. Administrative files documenting the operation of the facilities, including correspondence, minutes, annual and biennial reports, newsletters, and financial records also are found. Noninmate records of genealogical interest include personnel and payroll records before 1940.

*Access:* State Archives notebooks: name of city in which the facility is located. Various indexes are available. Access to certain records is restricted.

Reference Collections

Minnesota State Prison (Stillwater) Reports, 1861–84, listing all prisoners and their offenses. The reports for 1860–73 list every person who was paid by the prison for supplies and repairs. Reports for 1853–1900 list the names of prison officials. These reports are particularly useful, since most published materials do not give names of inmates.

*Access:* Catalog. For an every-name index to reports for 1853–1900, see Pope, *Minnesota Genealogical Index*, vol. 1 (Appendix 1: Genealogical Sources).

- **COUNTY HISTORIES** *see* Local and County Histories; Work Projects Administration (WPA) Resources

- **COUNTY RECORDS**                                     State Archives

  Naturalization records, assessment rolls, tax lists, petitions to establish roads, district and probate court records, poll lists, jail registers, welfare board minutes, coroners' records and records relating to the operation of county poor farms, tuberculosis sanatoriums, hospitals, and nursing homes. Before 1971 the county office of Superintendent of Schools monitored educational activities and compiled student censuses and educational information about pupils and teachers. Annual financial statements prepared by the County Auditor list all county expenditures, naming the persons and firms who were paid and for what. The Reference Collections holds some of these reports, as does the State Archives. The records vary from county to county.

  In general, land records, including deeds, mortgages, and grantee/grantor indexes, are retained by the County Recorder. Probate case files are retained by the Court Administrator in each county. Birth and death records recorded in the county from 1870 and marriage records recorded in the county from the time of its creation are retained with the Court Administrator or other county department to which that responsibility has been assigned by the county board. Divorce records, however, are in the court records in the State Archives.

  *Access:* State Archives notebooks: name of county. The records are arranged by county offices, courts, municipalities, and school districts, with Superintendent of Schools following school district records. Access status is noted in the main guide entries under the specific type of records (for example, Court Records; School Records).

- **COURT RECORDS** *see also* Bond and Oath Records; Business Records: Business Name Registrations; Coroners' Reports; Naturalization Records; Professional Certificates, Licenses, and Registrations

### Civil Case Files                                        State Archives

Documents relating to matters brought before the court, including monetary matters, changes of name, divorces, garnishments, and adoptions. The files may include complaint, answer, summons, findings, and judgment.

*Access:* State Archives notebooks: county name, District Court. The records are arranged by file number. Indexes generally remain in the county seat in the office of Court Administrator. Access to some records is restricted under state law.

### Criminal Case Files                                   State Archives

Documents relating to criminal proceedings, including murder, larceny, battery, and embezzlement charges. The individual files may contain warrants, subpoenas, verdicts, and sentencing information if the person was convicted. The State of Minnesota is listed as the plaintiff. Cases for some counties are interfiled with civil cases.

*Access:* State Archives notebooks: county name, District Court. Records are arranged by file number. Indexes generally remain in the county seat in the office of Court Administrator. Access to some records is restricted.

**C**

**Probate Records**                                          State Archives

Will books, final decrees of distribution of estate, and some order books, as well as indexes to wills and decrees. Records of insanity hearings and commitments from some probate courts are in the State Archives, as are letters of administration (usually pre-1880 only), minutes, records regarding guardianships and conservatorships, and wills from many county probate courts. While probate case files generally are retained by the courts, some from Freeborn, Pope, Washington, and Winona counties have been transferred to the State Archives.

Matters heard by the probate court in each county vary by jurisdiction and over time. Probate courts traditionally have had jurisdiction over settlements of estates and over guardianships of minors and incompetents (this has included insanity hearings and commitments). They formerly heard many family matters now handled by the family division of the district court.
*Access:* State Archives notebooks: county name, Probate Court. Many records are indexed. Access to insanity and juvenile records is restricted by law.

• **DAKOTA INDIANS: RESOURCES** *see* American Indians: Resources

• **DEATH RECORDS** *see* Appendix 3: Vital Records Repositories

• **DIARIES** *see* Personal Papers

• **DIRECTORIES**

**Business Directories**                                  Reference Collections

The major set of directories is R. L. Polk's *Gazetteer and Business Directory*, 1878–1926, which covers Minnesota in all volumes, and North Dakota, South Dakota, and Montana in the majority of them. Alphabetical arrangement by community name; in addition to names of individuals and their business category or firm name, information may include when community was established, location, and population. Each volume contains a reverse listing by business category. Many other individual business directories for the state or an individual city are also available, the earliest publication being dated 1865. These directories do not list employees of a business.
*Access:* Catalog: gazetteer or business directory.

**City Directories**                                       Reference Collections

Name listings of persons residing in city, with occupation and address; generally provided for large cities only. Some directories list removals to other cities as well as death dates. By 1930 city directories include a wife's name in the entry for her husband and a reverse listing under street address. The Reference Collections holds directories for the following Minnesota cities (beginning with year indicated): Albert Lea, 1914; Alexandria, 1911; Anoka, 1957; Austin/Mower County, 1894; Bemidji, 1922; Brainerd, 1888; Burnsville/Savage, 1967; Cloquet, 1927; Crookston, 1915; Duluth, 1882; Edina, 1930; Fairmont, 1957; Fargo/Moorhead, 1887; Faribault/Northfield/Rice County, 1907; Fergus Falls, 1919; Hastings, 1970; Hibbing, 1938; Hopkins, 1939; Hutchinson, 1972; International Falls, 1972; Little Falls, 1928; Mankato/Blue Earth County, 1878; Marshall, 1969; Minneapolis, 1859; Minneapolis suburban, 1956; New Ulm, 1911; Owatonna/Steele County, 1892; Pipestone, 1961; cities on the northern Minnesota iron ranges, 1912; Red Wing, 1876; Rochester/

Olmsted County, 1890; St. Cloud, 1888; St. Paul, 1856; St. Paul north suburban, 1956; St. Peter, 1971; South St. Paul/West St. Paul, 1947; Stillwater, 1881; Thief River Falls, 1915; Virginia, 1943; Willmar, 1907; Winona, 1866; and Worthington, 1969; as well as Sun Community Directories for many Minneapolis and St. Paul suburban areas, available from 1970s to present. Some directories include small communities within a larger city's vicinity, or all communities in the county, as well as farmers of the county. There are not complete sets of directories for every city. *The Dual City Blue Book* of 18 volumes (1885–1923) covers St. Paul and Minneapolis basically as a social register and includes a reverse directory by address.

In addition, the Reference Collections has an extensive collection of city directories from many of the larger communities of the United States. Not all major cities are represented and most of these are not full runs (i.e., every year published).
*Access:* Catalog: name of city—Directories.

### Professional Directories                                Reference Collections

State or national guides to members of professions, such as law or teaching. Often these directories list name, address, year of admittance or license for profession, college attended, and year of degree.
*Access:* Catalog: name of profession—Directories.

### Rural Directories                                        Reference Collections

Directories of farmers found as part of a county plat book (see section on plat books under Geographical Resources) or as part of county or city/county directory. The information may include name, section, township, number of acres, value of property, and post office. The Reference Collections has directories (beginning with the year indicated) for the following counties: Blue Earth, 1878 (see also Mankato); Brown, 1911 only; Carlton, 1927 only; Freeborn, 1914; Goodhue, 1894; Morrison, 1928 only; Mower, 1905 (see also Austin); Olmsted, 1896 (see also Rochester); Rice, 1907 (see also Faribault/Northfield); Stearns, 1931 only; Steele, 1892 (see also Owatonna); and Winona, 1923. In addition, some early gazetteers list farmers in selected Minnesota counties.
*Access:* Catalog: name of county—Directories.

### Telephone Directories                                    Reference Collections

The majority of telephone directories in the Reference Collections for Minnesota cities begin in the 1940–50 period with the exception of the one for St. Paul and Minneapolis, which began as a combined directory in 1915. Telephone directories for earlier years do not give as complete a listing of residents as do city directories, because telephones were not found in every home. The Reference Collections does not have telephone directories for non-Minnesota cities.
*Access:* Catalog: name of city—Directories.

### • DISASTER RELIEF RECORDS                                State Archives

Information about the Argyle hailstorm, 1886–87; seed grain program distribution requests (grasshopper relief), 1874; Chisholm fire relief, 1908; the Hinckley, Milaca, New York Mills, and Sandstone fires, 1894; and snowstorms, 1871–73. The information may include name of person requesting relief; locality; legal description of property; marital status and number of chil-

D

**D**

| No. | Name of sufferer | Locality of freezing. | | Nature of loss | | Other circumstances and remarks. |
|---|---|---|---|---|---|---|
| | | County | Township | In person | In property | |
| 10 | Patrick Condon age 45 | Meeker | Rice City | × Frozen to death | Stock badly damaged | Wife & 7 children. Destitute. |
| 11 | Mich'l J. Flynn Jr age 36 | Meeker | Rice City | × Frozen to death | One horse. | Wife & 6 children. Destitute. |
| 12 | Zacharias Flinsch age 42 | Brown | Home | × Frozen to death | One team of oxen | Wife & 1 child. Ill health & poor. |
| 13 | Nicholas Laux | Brown | Mulligan | —— | 2 teams oxen & 3 head cattle | Wife & 6 children. Owes for 1 team. Destitute. |
| 14 | Peter Zwaschka | Brown | Mulligan | —— | 1 team oxen & 5 head cattle | Wife & 1 child. |
| 15 | Francis Merz | Brown | Mulligan | —— | 1 yoke oxen, 4 head cattle, 6 sheep | Wife & 9 children (mostly large) |

*A page from the Disaster Relief Records of the Governor's Office lists persons who suffered in the severe Minnesota snowstorms of 1871–73.*

dren; nature of loss; plight of surviving family members; crops and livestock destroyed; photographs, plans, and specifications for replacement buildings; relief registrations; donations, amount of relief allowed, date of payment, in what manner paid, and remarks.

*Access:* State Archives notebooks: Governor, General and Miscellaneous Records, Disaster Relief Records.

### Drought Relief Applications
State Archives

Applications, 1933, with information about applicant's name; age; marital status; number at home in family; size of farm and terms of rental and/or mortgage status; value of personal property; livestock; auto; machinery; cash on hand; hay and grain in stock; debts; average monthly cream check; other income; number of bushels of corn, oats, barley; tons of hay; fuel for farm equipment; and other commodities being requested.

*Access:* State Archives notebooks: Executive Council. The records are arranged by county (a county with a large number of applicants may be subdivided by township).

### Hail Relief Applications
State Archives

Applications, 1930–34, with information about applicant's name, age, marital status, number at home in family, size of farm, value of personal property, livestock, auto, machinery, cash on hand, hay and grain in stock, debts, average monthly cream check, other income, number of bushels of crops, fuel for farm equipment, and other commodities being requested. Records for 1930 are for Marshall County only.

*Access:* State Archives notebooks: Executive Council. The records for 1931 are arranged by county. Those for 1932 and 1933 are alphabetical by surname within each county.

- **DIVORCE RECORDS** *see* Court Records: Civil Case Files.

- **DRAFT REGISTRATION LISTS** *see* Military and Veterans' Records

- **ELECTION RECORDS** *see also* County Records; Municipal Records; School Records: County Superintendent of Schools and School District Records; Township Records    State Archives

Affidavits of nomination, campaign expense statements with index to filings, election-contest records, abstracts of votes, and nominating petitions. These may give names of candidates, vote totals, office, campaign donations, and expense statements. Lists of registered voters are *not* included.

*Access:* State Archives notebooks: Secretary of State, Election Records. The records are arranged chronologically by election year, then by election (primary, general, and special).

- **ETHNIC RESOURCES** *see also* Newspapers; Oral Histories; Organizations Records; Religious Records

For detailed information about more than sixty ethnic groups who have lived in Minnesota, see Holmquist, ed., *They Chose Minnesota* (Appendix 1: Ethnic Sources).

- **FAMILY ASSOCIATIONS RECORDS**    Reference Collections

Newsletters, periodicals, and publications of Minnesota-based family associations and a limited collection of non-Minnesota associations. The items are cataloged as family history materials. Generally, newsletters describe activities of members, while periodicals have more substantial information, such as census records, biographies, ancestral charts, queries, and reminiscences.

*Access:* Catalog: surname. Some runs of periodicals have indexes that are noted in the cataloging information.

- **FAMILY HISTORIES**

Reference Collections

Approximately 15,000 family histories published in a variety of forms: typed, printed, mimeographed, computer-generated, and standard publisher's format. Ranging from a few pages to 1,000 or more, the histories cover families throughout the United States with emphasis on New England and the Midwest.

*Access:* Catalog: surname. The Reference Collections has almost 95 percent of the about 800 titles (the majority being family histories) listed in *The American Genealogical-Biographical Index* (published 1952–   ; available in the Reference Collections). About 1,300 unique titles (including many limited-edition, local family histories) held by the Reference Collections are listed in *A Complement to Genealogies in the Library of Congress: A Bibliography*, compiled and edited by Marion J. Kaminkow (Baltimore: Magna Carta Book

Company, 1981; 1,118 p.; available in the Reference Collections). The histories are *not* available through Interlibrary Loan.

Manuscripts Collections

Genealogical records collected by individual researchers. These may include ancestor charts, family group sheets, correspondence, photographs, maps, vital statistics, newspaper clippings, autobiographies, greeting cards, and family histories. The records may be originals, photocopies, or microfilms.
*Access:* Manuscripts Collections catalog: Genealogy; Family History; surname.

• **FARM CROP AND LABOR REPORTS**  State Archives

Reports include name of farmer, address, nearest shipping point, name of railroad, nationality or descent of farmer, kind of crops and acres planted in 1917 and 1918, livestock and number of each kind, number of silos, and report of farm labor needs.
*Access:* State Archives notebooks: Public Safety Commission, Farm Crop and Labor Reports. The records are arranged by county, then alphabetically by surname of farmer.

• **FEDERAL DOCUMENTS** *see* United States Government Documents

• **FINNISH AMERICANS, RESOURCES** *see* Ethnic Resources; Oral Histories, Appendix 1: Ethnic Sources

• **FIRE INSURANCE MAPS** *see* Geographical Resources

• **FRATERNAL ORGANIZATIONS RECORDS** *see* Organizations Records

• **FUR TRADE RECORDS** *see* Business Records: Fur Trade

• **GAZETTEERS** *see* Directories: Business Directories; Geographical Resources

• **GENEALOGICAL ORGANIZATIONS PUBLICATIONS**
Reference Collections

Periodicals and books published by the Minnesota Genealogical Society (MGS), genealogical organizations from around Minnesota, and the majority of the state genealogical organizations in the United States. Of particular interest is a periodical published by the MGS, the *Minnesota Genealogist* (see Appendix 1: Genealogical Sources). The MGS (founded in 1969) has also published several volumes of ancestor and family-group charts noting the ancestral lines of some of its members, as well as the booklet *Introduction to Minnesota Research Sources*, compiled by Warren and Peterson (see Appendix 1: Genealogical Sources). For more information about genealogical organizations in Minnesota, see Appendix 3.
*Access:* Catalog: name of society and the state or subject of major interest.

• **GEOGRAPHICAL RESOURCES** *see also* Land Records
Map Collections

A collection of about 37,000 individual maps and 1,600 atlases. The emphasis is on Minnesota and the Midwest, but with selected reference maps and atlases for a wider geographical area. A major part of the collection is comprised of publicly and privately published, individual maps of Minnesota Territory and the state of Minnesota and its regions, counties, and cities. Although they are fairly general, these maps show the development of the area's political boundaries and transportation network, along with the spread of both urban and rural settlement. Of particular use to genealogists are the locations of many cities, towns, and villages that no longer exist and can be found only in gazetteers and place-name guides.

*Access:* Map Collections catalogs.

### Fire Insurance Maps                                 Map Collections

Fire insurance maps and urban atlases for large urban areas, cities, towns, and villages. The atlases for Minneapolis, St. Paul, and Duluth (from the mid-1880s to the 1940s) cover the totality of the corporate limits, show most structures (including residences, industrial sites, and commercial buildings), and give legal descriptions of lots and blocks, with some building numbers.

Insurance maps and atlases of more than 950 Minnesota towns and cities provide — for built-up areas of a city — detailed renderings of buildings and include information about building location and address, building material, function of building, number of stories, porches, outbuildings, and identification as a private dwelling or a rental property. Commercial designations, such as saloon or law office, are indicated, and schools, churches, and halls are identified. Publication dates range from the mid-1880s to the 1970s. Insurance maps and atlases of the Sanborn Map Publishing Company are available on microfilm for research and copying.

*Access:* Map Collections catalogs.

### Gazetteers                                         Reference Collections

Place-name guides for Minnesota, other states, and foreign countries. Entries may include original plat date, origin of name, and other historical information. The standard guide for Minnesota is Upham, *Minnesota Geographic Names* (see Appendix 1: Minnesota Historical Sources).

*Access:* Catalog: name of state or country.

### Plat Books                                         Map Collections

Maps and atlases that show land ownership by county and may include county histories, directories and biographies of farmers and landowners, urban plats, and photographs and other illustrations. This information was obtained from land ownership records in the offices of the County Registers of Deeds and from canvassings of the counties. Publication dates are irregular. The collection includes more than 500 county atlases for Minnesota from the 1860s to the present and about 200 county atlases from other parts of the country, mostly New England, the Midwest, North Dakota, and South Dakota. For a bibliography of Minnesota county atlases, see Treude, *Windows to the Past* (Appendix 1: Minnesota Historical Sources).

*Access:* Map Collections catalogs: name of county. Pre-1914 Minnesota atlases are on microfilm and available through Interlibrary Loan.

### Post Office Location Guides                        Reference Collections

The principal published list of post offices in Minnesota is Patera and Gallagher, *Post Offices of Minnesota* (see Appendix 1: Minnesota Historical Sources). The information for each post office includes the date of establishment and of discontinuance, if appropriate. The list is indexed by county and name of post office. A post office card file compiled by Newton D. Mereness notes any early changes of post office name and the name of first postmaster in each community.

*Access:* Catalog for list; ask staff for assistance with card file.

For the United States, the major guides are the *U.S. Official Register* (1831–1911) and the *U.S. Official Postal Guide* (1851–1978).

*Access:* Ask staff for assistance.

# G

**Topographic Maps**                                                              Map Collections

Federally produced topographic map set of Minnesota in detailed scale. More than 1,700 sheets cover the state. Most were produced after World War II and contain information about the physical lay of the land and such cultural features as individual farms, small villages and towns, rural churches, and cemetery locations. They are often the only street maps available for many urban places. Many of the names on these maps are those in local usage, and often their sources are previously published maps and historical publications. Therefore, many names remain on the maps long after they have disappeared as functional places.

*Access:* Map Collections guide sheets.

**Township Organization Records** *see also* Township Records

State Archives

Record books and files giving information about the organization of Minnesota townships and villages, including names, name changes, locations (legal descriptions), and dates and nature of any changes in name, boundaries, or organizational status.

*Access:* State Archives notebooks: Auditor, Township Organization Records.

*The Coyn family sailed back to the United States after a visit to relatives in Ireland during the 1930s. Members of the family had immigrated about the time of World War I.*

**Ward Maps**                                    State Archives; Reference Collections

Available for major cities, such as St. Paul, Minneapolis, Duluth, Rochester, and Winona. Wards changed over time, but these maps are still very useful when researching in the unindexed census records of these cities.
*Access:* Ask staff for assistance.

- **GOVERNOR'S OFFICE RECORDS** *see also* Disaster Relief Records; Professional Certificates, Licenses, and Registrations

**Appointment Records**                                    State Archives

Records of appointments to state boards, commissions, and departments; appointments of judges; and other appointments giving name of person, name of office, date of appointment, and expiration date.
*Access:* State Archives notebooks: Governor, General and Miscellaneous Records, Appointment Records. Indexes cover 1898–1953.

**Citizenship Restoration Records**                                    State Archives

Certificates sent to the governor, 1889–1963, by wardens, superintendents, officials, and judges affirming the rights of persons to restoration of citizenship following completion of prison or reformatory sentences, suspended sentences, or probation periods. The records may have name, date of conviction, nature of crime, date of sentence, in what court sentenced, and date of release.
*Access:* State Archives notebooks: Governor, General and Miscellaneous Records, Citizenship Restoration Records. The records are arranged chronologically, then alphabetically for each type of certificate.

- **GRAND ARMY OF THE REPUBLIC (GAR) RECORDS** *see* Military and Veterans' Records

- **HISPANIC AMERICANS: RESOURCES** *see* Ethnic Resources; Oral Histories; Appendix 1: Ethnic Sources

- **HOSPITAL RECORDS** *see also* Military and Veterans' Records: Veterans' Facility Records; Poor Farm Records

**Private Health and Welfare Facilities Records**          Manuscripts Collections

Records of many private health and welfare institutions, about the institutions themselves and their patients. Examples of such collections are the records for Abbott Northwestern Hospital (Minneapolis), Fairview Deaconess Hospital School of Nursing (Minneapolis), Maternity Hospital of Minneapolis, Babies Home of St. Paul, and Edward F. Waite Neighborhood House (Minneapolis). The records may contain admission and discharge registers, administrative records governing the operations of the facility, and financial records. Patient registers of St. Paul (Luther) Hospital and Ellsworth (Minnesota) Hospital are in the records of the Minnesota Department of Health in the State Archives.
*Access:* Manuscripts Collections catalog: name of city in which the facility is located or appropriate general subject heading (for example, Children—Charities or Social Services). Access to certain records may be restricted.

# G-H

Records of state facilities for the care of the mentally retarded, mentally handicapped, chemically dependent, criminally insane, and physically handicapped. Facilities include the regional treatment centers (formerly called state hospitals) at Anoka (1900–   ), Brainerd (1957–   ), Cambridge (1925–   ), Faribault (1979–   ), Fergus Falls (1887–   ), Moose Lake (1938–   ), St. Peter (1866–   ), and Willmar (1907–   ); the former state hospitals at Rochester (1879–1982), Hastings (1900–1978), Owatonna (1945–70), and Sandstone (1950–59); and the Gillette Hospital for Crippled Children (St. Paul; 1897–   ). The records vary from facility to facility, but may include admission and discharge registers; patient case books before 1900; hospital or clinic registers; birth and death records; cemetery records; autopsy reports; population reports; and, occasionally, commitment papers. Administrative records may include minutes; annual and biennial reports; executive correspondence; summary financial records; facility publications; and operating records. Nonresident records may include personnel and payroll records before 1940.

## H-L

The State Archives also has records of former tubercular sanatoriums, including the Minnesota State Sanatorium at Ah-Gwah-Ching (Walker, 1907–   ) and the Glen Lake Sanatorium in Minnetonka (1916–91; after 1963, Glen Lake also was known as the Oak Terrace Nursing Home and was operated by the Minnesota Department of Human Services; Oak Terrace closed on June 30, 1991; its records are in the State Archives). Other sanatoriums operated by counties or groups of counties for which records are available include Buena Vista Sanatorium (Wabasha, 1917–55), Nopeming Sanatorium (St. Louis County, 1912–71), Southwestern Minnesota Sanatorium (Worthington, 1915–73), Sunnyrest Sanatorium (Crookston, 1913–67), and Riverside Sanatorium (Granite Falls, 1915–73). Sanatorium records may contain admission and discharge registers, annual and biennial reports, financial records, and minutes of the government authority. Occasionally, the records may include payrolls.

*Access:* State Archives notebooks: name of city; name of facility; county name, name of facility. Access to certain health and welfare records is restricted.

- **INDIANS: RESOURCES** *see* American Indians: Resources

- **INSURANCE MAPS** *see* Geographical Resources: Fire Insurance Maps

- **JAIL RECORDS** *see* Correctional Facilities Records

- **JEWISH AMERICANS: RESOURCES** *see* Ethnic Resources; Oral Histories; Religious Records; Appendix 1: Religious Sources

- **JUSTICE OF THE PEACE RECORDS** *see* Municipal Records; Township Records

- **LABOR: RESOURCES** *see* Newspapers; Oral Histories; Union Records

- **LAND RECORDS** *see also* Geographical Resources; Railroad Records

The acquisition, sale, and management of Minnesota's trust fund, railroad grant, and related lands, as well as the federal land survey of Minnesota and the initial transfer of title of public lands to the state or to private parties are documented in large part in records in the State Archives, in microfilm

*The Minneapolis-New Ulm Bowling Club had a picnic on June 19, 1900.*

produced by the MHS, or in records scheduled to be transferred to the State Archives. Some key records, notably United States General Land Office land patent records, are in the National Archives.

Because of the variety and complexity of these records, they are not described in this guide except for Original Entry Tract Books, Registers of Land Entries, and Rural Credit Department Records (see below). See also Kinney and Lucas, *Guide to the Records of Minnesota's Public Lands* (Appendix 1: Minnesota Historical Sources).

### Original Entry Tract Books                                State Archives

Books created by the United States General Land Office, and later transferred to state custody. They provide a consolidated record of the initial transfer of title from the United States to private parties or to the state, regardless of how the land was acquired (by homestead, preemption, scrip, or grant). For each parcel of land, the following information is recorded: price, original purchaser or transferee, number of the homestead certificate or other authorizing document, sale date, date the final patent (title) was issued, name of patentee, and citation to the entry in the land patent records in the United States General Land Office records, National Archives. Land transfers are recorded by range and township.

*Access:* State Archives notebooks: U.S. General Land Office, Original Entry Tract Books. An index organized by range and township can help researchers locate information about specific land parcels in the tract books. Both the tract books and the index are in microform and available through Interlibrary Loan.

### Registers of Land Entries                                State Archives

Records of the United States General Land Office districts documenting the acquisition of state land by cash purchase, various types of scrip, military bounty land warrants, under the provisions of the Homestead or Timber Culture acts, or of ceded Indian lands. These records may be variously titled Register of Entries, Register of Certificates to Purchasers, Register of Homestead Entries, Register of Final Homestead Certificates, Register of Military Bounty Land Warrant Entries, or Serial Registers. Although these records focus on the details of the land transaction itself, they also place the purchaser in a specific place at a specific time. Some contain brief amounts of personal information about the purchaser. Additional biographical information may be found among the Registrars' and Receivers' correspondence of the land districts, especially when the validity of the entries was contested.

*Access:* State Archives notebooks: U.S. General Land Office, individual land district and record series.

**Rural Credit Department Records**                                   State Archives

The Rural Credit Department (1923–73) loaned money to farmers threatened by loss of their land during the Great Depression. Farmers were given the opportunity to repay loans slowly. The incomplete records in the State Archives include real estate loan records, loan records cards, sales journals, lease records, and contract for deed files. Genealogical information is limited to farm histories, correspondence regarding ownership, and financial information on the farm and its produce.

*Access:* State Archives notebooks: Rural Credit Department.

- **LICENSES** *see* Motor Vehicle and Driver's License Registration Records; Professional Certificates, Licenses, and Registrations

- **LOCAL AND COUNTY HISTORIES** *see also* Work Projects Administration (WPA) Resources

                                    Manuscripts Collections; State Archives

Manuscript histories generally written by residents, telling the history of a community or county. They may include interviews with early settlers, photographs, cemetery transcriptions, and listings of town and/or county officials.
*Access:* Manuscripts Collections catalog: name of town and/or county; name of town, Work Projects Administration. State Archives notebooks: county and township or city.

                                                      Reference Collections

Published histories comprise the most extensive collection of materials about Minnesota's counties, cities, villages, and townships. Many were published before 1920 or as part of the celebration of the United States bicentennial in 1976. A number of counties have no major published history. Significant holdings of local history materials are available for states in New England, the Western Reserve, the Midwest, and the Northwest—all areas notable in the migrations of Minnesotans. The histories vary in scope, period of time, and quality. For a bibliography of Minnesota county atlases (which sometimes contain local-history information), see Treude, *Windows to the Past* (Appendix 1: Minnesota Historical Sources).
*Access:* Catalog: name of community. Some histories are indexed. If biographical sketches are included, they may be arranged or indexed alphabetically.

- **MAPS** *see* Geographical Resources

- **MARRIAGE RECORDS** *see* Religious Records; Vital Records; Appendix 3: Vital Records Repositories

- **MEDICAL EXAMINERS' RECORDS** *see* Coroners' Records; Coroners' Reports

- **MEXICAN AMERICANS: RESOURCES** *see* Ethnic Resources; Oral Histories; Appendix 1: Ethnic Sources

- **MILITARY AND VETERANS' RECORDS**

Reference Collections

Rosters for the Revolutionary and Civil wars comprise the bulk of the published military records held in the Reference Collections, with a smaller number of items for the French and Indian Wars, the War of 1812, the Mexican-American War, the Spanish-American War, and World War I. In addition to published rosters, a special Civil War veterans file was compiled to augment the information about Minnesotans who served in Minnesota regiments and to identify those who served with other states before moving to Minnesota after the war. This information may include residence, death date, widow's name, pension file number, regiment, and company. The Reference Collections also includes many general histories of the wars.

*Access:* Ask staff for assistance. A limited number of the rosters are adequately indexed; the majority are arranged by regiment name or number and then by company. Rosters of men who served in Minnesota units during the Civil War and the Dakota War (Sioux Uprising) of 1862 are indexed.

State Archives; Manuscripts Collections

Records may include bonus correspondence, daybooks, descriptive lists, hospital reports, inspection reports, lists of commissioned and noncommissioned officers, military appointments, military service record cards, monthly returns, muster rolls, payrolls and certificates of payments, pension information, orders, quartermaster's records, records of casualties, registers of men transferred, registers of men discharged, registers of deaths, registers of deserters, resignations and discharges, and miscellaneous information. The records include information for the Mexican-American War, the Civil War, the Dakota War (Sioux Uprising) of 1862, the Indian wars, the Spanish-American War, the Mexican Border Service, World War I, the Minnesota Home Guard, the Minnesota State Militia, and the Minnesota National Guard. Records may give person's hair and eye color, height, weight, place of birth, service unit, and ranking.

*Access:* Ask staff for assistance. Most records are not indexed, and many are in poor physical condition.

### Grand Army of the Republic (GAR) Records

State Archives

Central office files of the Minnesota Department of the GAR, an organization of men who served in the Union army and navy during the Civil War, plus records for many of the almost 200 individual posts established in the state between the 1880s and 1940s. Central office files include post charters and organizational records, departmental correspondence, membership information, encampment (reunion) files, and death reports (incomplete, 1889–1920) received from individual posts. The records of posts include minutes of meetings, registers of members, personal narratives, descriptive books detailing the war service of members, correspondence, and post financial records.

*Access:* State Archives notebooks: Grand Army of the Republic.

*Civil War soldier Henry O. ("Harry") Fifield was drum major of the renowned First Minnesota Volunteer Infantry Regiment that saw action in the battles of Bull Run, Antietam, and Gettysburg.*

MHS GENEALOGICAL
RESOURCES

Annual reports of GAR encampments—complete for Minnesota (1881–1947), with miscellaneous reports for other states and national encampments. The reports describe activities of member posts, list officers, and note deaths occuring during the year, giving name of person, date of death, residence, and post, with an occasional biographical sketch. Publications of the Ladies of the Grand Army of the Republic auxiliary are also available.

*Access:* Catalog.

# M

### Military Service Record Cards
State Archives

Service record cards for persons who entered federal military service via the Minnesota State Militia and the Minnesota National Guard. The information recorded may include name, service number, where and when enrolled, age or birth date, birthplace, residence, dates and places of service, service unit, rank or rating, where and when discharged, and civilian occupation. Included are records for the Civil War, the Spanish-American War (all branches of service), World War I (all branches, including nurses), the state guard, and the National Guard.

*Access:* State Archives notebooks: Adjutant General. The records are on microfilm and available through Interlibrary Loan; they are grouped by war and service branch, then alphabetically by surname within each group.

### Muster Rolls
State Archives

Individual serviceman's name, date and place of enlistment, physical characteristics, date and place of discharge, age, amount paid, clothes provided, and remarks. Muster rolls for the Civil and Spanish-American wars are included, along with a few for World War I.

*Access:* State Archives notebooks: Adjutant General, name of war. The records are not indexed. They are fragile and their availability is limited.

### Pension Records Indexes
Reference Collections

Available published indexes are:

> National Genealogical Society. *Index of Revolutionary War Pension Applications* (Washington, D.C.: National Genealogical Society, 1966; 1,324 p.)
>
> White, Virgil D. *Index to Old Wars Pension Files: 1815–1926* (2 vols.; Waynesboro, Tenn.: National Historical Publishing Company, 1987)
>
> United States War Department. *Letter from the Secretary of War Transmitting a Report of the Names, Rank, and Line, of Every Person Placed on the Pension List, in Pursuance of the Act of the 18th March, 1818* (1820; reprint, Baltimore: Southern Book Company, 1955; 672 p.)
>
> United States Congress, Senate. *Report from the Secretary of War . . . in Relation to the Pension Establishment of the United States* (23rd Cong., 1st sess., 1835, S. Doc. 514, Serials 249–51)
>
> Genealogical Society of Utah, Salt Lake City. *A General Index to a Census of Pensioners for Revolutionary or Military Service 1840* (Baltimore: Genealogical Publishing Company, 1965; 382 p.)
>
> United States Congress, Senate. *List of Pensioners on the Roll: January 1, 1883* (47th Cong., 2nd sess., 1882–83, S. Doc. 84, Serials

2078–82; pensioners with Minnesota addresses are listed in Serial 2081, p. 531–91).

*Access:* Catalog.

## Pension Registers
State Archives

Pension registers and indexes, about 1877–1949, for Minnesotans receiving pensions for military service, listing claimant's name, date of filing, address, military unit, information to support claim, action on claim. Many applications were filed by widows or children of servicemen.

*Access:* State Archives notebooks: Adjutant General, Pension Registers and Indexes and Pension Registers, Indian Wars. All but one of the 28 volumes are indexed.

## Soldiers Bonus Records
State Archives

Applications to the Soldiers Bonus Board from Minnesota soldiers, marines, sailors, and medical personnel who served in World War I. The 51-question form includes veteran's name, place and date of birth, name and residence of closest relative, draft information, present residence and occupation, name of employer and business address, name and address of parents at time of enlistment, length of residence in Minnesota, and marital status.

*Access:* State Archives notebooks: Treasurer, Soldiers Bonus Warrant Record and Soldiers Bonus Applications. The applications are arranged by application number. The application number for an individual veteran may be found under the veteran's name in the four unindexed volumes of the Soldiers Bonus Warrant Record.

## Veterans' Facility Records
State Archives

Resident and administration records for the state-operated Minnesota Veterans Home in Minneapolis (established 1887), including admission and discharge records, histories of residents' military service, hospital and clinic records, and population reports. Administration records document the governance and operation of the veterans' home; they include minutes, annual and biennial reports, superintendent's correspondence, and summary financial records. Nonresident records include pre-1940 personnel and payroll records.

*Access:* State Archives notebooks: Soldiers Home. Access to certain records may be restricted.

## Veterans' Organizations Records
State Archives; Manuscripts Collections

Information about members of service units and activities, residences of members since military service, and women's auxiliaries. The records may include applications for membership, obituaries of deceased members, biographical sketches, names and service records of members, personal narratives, reunion materials, and annual-meeting materials.

*Access:* State Archives notebooks: Adjutant General, name of organization. Manuscripts Collections catalog: name of organization; name of military conflict; names of officers of organization; name of person. The records are generally not indexed.

## World War I Draft Registration Lists
State Archives

Copies of the original draft lists from the United States War Department. The lists have the names, addresses, and draft numbers of 540,000 Minnesota men registered under the draft.

M

*Access:* State Archives notebooks: War Records Commission, Draft Registration Lists. The records are arranged by county and local draft board. They are not indexed and are difficult to read.

### World War I Induction Lists                                    State Archives

Photostatic copies of the original induction lists, covering about 60 percent of the 80,000 Minnesota men called into service under the draft. The information includes induction number, name, date ordered to report, date and hour person reported, date forwarded to and reported at mobilization camp, date if failed to report at mobilization camp, date rejected, and date of final acceptance.

*Access:* State Archives notebooks: War Records Commission, Induction Lists. The records are arranged by county, local draft board, and date. They are not indexed and are difficult to read.

### World War I Military Records                                   State Archives

Biographical information and military service records for Minnesota men and women who served in World War I. The World War I Military Service Record, a four-page form voluntarily compiled by the individual, gives biographical information and military service record, including occupation before entry into military and activities upon return to civilian life. The Gold Star Roll Record, a four-page form voluntarily compiled by family members, gives biographical information and military service records for men and women who died in service, including occupation before entry into military, and information about date, place, and cause of death.

*Access:* State Archives notebooks: War Records Commission, World War I Military Service Records; Public Safety Commission, Gold Star Roll Records. Alphabetical arrangement.

### World War II Military Records                                  State Archives

Records of military service, about 1941–47, for men who were commissioned, enlisted, or inducted into the armed services during World War II. Information includes name, address, local board number, register number, date and place of birth, race, branch of armed services, dates of entry into and separation from the armed services. As of 1991, records held for Rice, Waseca, and Watonwan counties and local draft board nos. 14–25 of Hennepin County, covering northeast, north, and south Minneapolis, and some western and northwestern suburban areas.

*Access:* State Archives notebooks: Hennepin County, Selective Service Record Cards, arrangement by board number, then alphabetical with each local board; Rice County, War History Committee, alphabetical arrangement; Waseca County, War History Committee, alphabetical arrangement by surname; Watonwan County, Selective Service Board, alphabetical arrangement by first letter of surname. Researcher should check other counties in State Archives notebooks to determine if similar records have been received since 1991.

- **MINNESOTA HISTORIC RESOURCES SURVEY: MANUSCRIPTS**
                                                    Manuscripts Collections

Survey forms for the manuscripts held by county and local historical societies in Minnesota, compiled by the MHS, 1973–79. The survey lists and describes primary source materials and printed materials of local significance, including directories, maps, clippings, reference files, historical research papers, and sound and visual resources. All county historical societies participated with the exceptions of the Olmsted County Historical Society and the St. Louis County Historical Society. The form gives name of repository; collection title, inclusive dates, and accession number; donor's name and address; date the collection was received; information about the primary person or organization documented in the collection; any restrictions on access; information about the collection's physical condition, size, arrangement, storage, and record types; and a summary of its contents.

*Access:* Manuscripts Collections catalog. The records are arranged alphabetically by county and, within each county, alphabetically by the name of the repository. The set of survey forms is on microfilm and available through Interlibrary Loan.

M

- **MOTOR VEHICLE AND DRIVER'S LICENSE REGISTRATION RECORDS**

State Archives

Register of motor vehicles (1909–14, 1921) includes vehicle number and description, and owner's name and residence. Records of chauffeurs (1909–11) include name, city and county of residence, and date of registration. Motorcycle registrations (1909–13) include vehicle number and description, and owner's name with city and county of residence.

*Access:* State Archives notebooks: Secretary of State, Motor Vehicle Division. The records are not indexed.

- **MUNICIPAL RECORDS**

State Archives

Records of more than 400 of the state's 855 municipalities. (After 1975 all villages became known as cities by legislative mandate. Municipality is the for-

*Rudolph Runez and automobile in 1925*

mal title given to cities of all sizes.) Sets of municipal records vary in their completeness both in date spans and in record types.

The records include such administrative information as city council minutes, annual reports, correspondence and subject files; financial records, including payroll registers and registers of receipts and disbursements; municipal court and justice of the peace dockets; cemetery records, including burial registers and lot owner records; police jail registers and registers of tramps lodged in jail; death records; scrapbooks and newsletters; and poll lists and election registers containing the names of persons who voted in elections. Notable among the latter are Minneapolis registers of electors for 1902–23, containing significant genealogical information. Some municipal records include information about the registration or licensing of saloonkeepers, peddlers, and others. Names of city council members appear in the minutes, and names of city officials and staff can be found in payroll registers and annual reports.

*Access:* State Archives notebooks: name of county, city, or village.

- **NATURALIZATION RECORDS**                                  State Archives

First papers (declaration of intention, petition, application, and registry) and final papers (oath, petition, and certificate) required for persons applying for U.S. citizenship. Records before 1906 include name, date of filing, present residence in state, previous residence by state or country, renunciation of former allegiance, oath of allegiance, and witnesses' names. The record may include the date and port of entry into the United States. A standard form established in 1906 required more specific information about the person: personal description, names of wife and children, place of birth, place of residence, and date and location of entry into the United States. In 1922 changes in federal law enabled a wife to obtain her own citizenship independent of her husband's.

*Access:* State Archives notebooks: name of county, District Court; Minnesota Supreme Court. There are various indexes to the records. Records for many counties are on microfilm and available through Interlibrary Loan.

- **NEGRO AMERICANS: RESOURCES** *see* Ethnic Resources; Oral Histories: Appendix 1: Ethnic Sources

- **NEWSPAPERS**                                         Newspaper Collections

Daily and weekly Minnesota newspapers, as well as non-English-language, labor, ethnic, reservation (*The Progress* and *The Tomahawk* of the White Earth Indian Reservation for the Ojibway), legal, prison (the *Prison Mirror* of the Minnesota State Prison, Stillwater), religious, political, school, and other special-interest papers. Since 1957 legal newspapers (those publishing or carrying legal notices) have been required to file copies with the MHS. Approximately 95 percent of the collection of more than 3,000 titles has been microfilmed, although a number of small-town newspapers are still in bound volumes. The completeness of an individual newspaper file varies with the city and the time period. For information about the names, locations, and publishing histories of Minnesota newspapers, see *Gale Directory of Publications and Broadcast Media;* Gregory, *American Newspapers;* and Hage, *Newspapers on the Minnesota Frontier* (Appendix 1: Minnesota Historical Sources); and Littlefield and Parins, *American Indian and Alaska Native Newspapers and Periodicals* (Appendix 1: Ethnic Sources).

*In August 1937 a resident of Funkley learned the news from the* Minneapolis Tribune *in a general store. This picture was taken by Russell Lee, a documentary photographer for the Farm Security Administration, a federal agency that sponsored rural programs during the Great Depression.*

Generally, small-town newspapers publish more detailed obituaries that may include the places and dates of birth and marriage, survivors, and biographical information. In larger cities, particularly Minneapolis and St. Paul, the older daily newspapers did not publish obituaries as they do today. If a death notice was printed, it was more often a notice of only the funeral.

*Access:* Newspaper Collections: notebooks: name of county, name of city, title of newspaper. There are also separate lists for some of the special-interest newspapers. There is no separate master index of obituaries published in Minnesota newspapers. The Biography Files in the Reference Collections (see Biographical Records: Biography Files) have many references to newspaper obituaries. Knowing the date and place of death will help to locate obituaries for persons not listed in the Biography Files. Combined, printed indexes are available for the following newspapers (here referred to by commonly known titles): the *Minnesota Pioneer* (1849–52); the *Minneapolis Star* and the *Minneapolis Tribune* (1971–80); the *Star Tribune* of Minneapolis (1981–86); the *St. Paul Pioneer Press* and the *St. Paul Dispatch* (1967–    ); and the *Duluth Herald* and the *Duluth News Tribune* (1978–    ). Microfilms of many newspapers are available through Interlibrary Loan (ILL) and for purchase. For information about microfilms, ILL, and newspaper research by mail, see Appendix 2: Services. Manuscripts Collections has the Babcock Newspaper Index, which includes selected articles from early Minnesota newspapers, primarily of the 1849–59 period. Some of the subjects covered are travel, immigration, and the rise and decline of towns.

- **NURSING HOME RECORDS** *see* Hospital Records; Poor Farm Records

- **OBITUARIES** *see* Biographical Records; Newspapers; Pioneer Settlers Obituaries and Index

- **OJIBWAY INDIANS: RESOURCES** *see* American Indians: Resources

- **ORAL HISTORIES**  Sound and Visual Collections; Manuscripts Collections

More than 1,500 interviews with Minnesotans from all walks of life—from politicians and business leaders to farmers, labor leaders, and members of the state's major ethnic communities. Information about family life, holiday customs, immigration, and community activities is represented throughout the collection, especially in the autobiographical reminiscences. Special projects document facets of the Asian, Black, Finnish, Jewish, Mexican, Scandinavian, labor, and church communities in Minnesota. Other projects focus on industrial and environmental history and on a major powerline construction controversy in the 1970s.

Tapes for listening as well as many oral-history transcriptions are available for use in the Research Center.

*Access:* Sound and Visual Collections catalog: names of oral history narrators and major subjects. Manuscripts Collections catalog: Oral History; detailed information about each interview is available. For a thorough name, place, and subject index, see Cuff and Fogerty, comps, *Oral History Collections of the Minnesota Historical Society* (Appendix 1: Guides to Collections of the MHS). Access to certain interviews is restricted.

- **ORGANIZATIONS RECORDS**

Manuscripts Collections

*Wing Young Huie and his mother, Lee Ngook Kum Huie, in Duluth about 1960. Wing Young participated in an oral history interview in 1979 for a project about Asian Americans in Minnesota.*

Information about members, residences of members, and activities of a variety of organizations—social, ethnic, fraternal, patriotic, and service-oriented. The records may include applications, biographical sketches, obituaries, organizational activities, and additional materials. Some records are in languages other than English.

*Access:* Manuscripts Collections catalog: name of organization, names of officers of organization, or name of person. Records are not indexed.

Reference Collections

A collection of publications by various types of organizations: specific ethnic groups, such as the St. Andrew's Society (Scots); fraternal societies, which often grew out of insurance cooperatives, such as the Modern Woodmen of America; patriotic organizations, such as the Daughters of the American Revolution (DAR); religious organizations, such as the Knights of Columbus; and service organizations, such as Rotary International.

The publications may be newsletters, annual reports, membership lists, histories, or constitutions and bylaws. They vary in format, frequency, and type of information included. Annual reports may have biographical information or obituaries of recently deceased members. Membership lists may also note addresses or death dates. Newsletters often mention members' activities. Publications of patriotic organizations often include all of the above as well as information about ancestors.

The Reference Collections has lineage books for the DAR, the Sons of the American Revolution, the Colonial Dames, the Ladies of the Grand Army of the Republic, the Mayflower Descendants, and other patriotic organizations.

*Access:* Catalog: name of organization; Swiss-American, German-American, etc.; Swiss in Minnesota, Germans in Minnesota, etc.

*Members of Croatian Lodge No. 128, H.Z.I., in South St. Paul, about 1916. This leading Croatian fraternal group started in Pittsburgh as Hrvatska Zajednica u Sjedinjenim Državama (the Croatian Union of the United States) in 1894.*

## • ORPHAN TRAINS

Between the 1850s and the 1920s, some orphaned or otherwise homeless children were removed from the East Coast to other areas of the United States for placing out in homes where they received care and education in exchange for labor. (The trains in which they traveled were actually only one or two reserved passenger cars.) Chiefly responsible was the New York Children's Aid Society (NYCAS), which sent 340 children to Minnesota, most within a three-year period in the 1880s; all were placed in seven southern counties. Placement records are at the NYCAS. The MHS Reference Collections has only a few volumes of NYCAS published annual reports and some information in the vertical files. Researchers are encouraged to contact the Orphan Train Heritage Society of America, 4453 South 48th, Springdale, AR 72764.

## • PASSENGER SHIP LISTS                    Reference Collections

Indexes to many printed passenger lists, some of which are in the Reference Collections. Since Minnesota was not a first port of arrival, there are no federal records of passengers arriving at Minnesota ports. Steamboats arriving in Minnesota were not required to deposit passenger lists with any governmental agency; however, some steamboat passenger arrivals are listed in newspapers published in the cities where the passengers debarked.

*Access:* Catalog: Ships—Passenger Lists; Steamboat Lines—Passenger Lists. About 10 percent of the available passenger lists are indexed in *Passenger and Immigration Lists Index: A Guide to Published Arrival Records of about 500,000 Passengers Who Came to the United States and Canada in the Seventeenth, Eighteenth, and Nineteenth Centuries,* edited by P. William Filby (3 vols., 7 suppls.; Detroit: Gale Research Company, 1981–88). Many of the published books and periodical articles indexed in Filby's guide are available in the Reference Collections.

- **PATRIOTIC ORGANIZATIONS RECORDS** *see* Organizations Records

- **PENSION RECORDS** *see* Military and Veterans' Records; Teachers Retirement Association Records

- **PERSONAL PAPERS**                                        Manuscripts Collections

  Hundreds of collections, each of which may include correspondence, diaries, account books, reminiscences, autograph albums, photographs, scrapbooks, and genealogies. A Minnesotan is always represented in each collection, but family and friends may be from elsewhere.

  *Access:* Manuscripts Collections catalog: name of person or family surname. For published guides, see Appendix 1: Guides to Collections of the MHS.

- **PHOTOGRAPHS**

  **Community Photographs**                                  Sound and Visual Collections

  Postcards, snapshots, news photos, and commercial studio photos from 1850 to the present, taken in every Minnesota county and most towns. Photographs of the town where a person settled or grew up can be evocative when creating a family history. Occasionally, photos may be found of the business or industry in which a person worked, or the school or place of worship attended.

  For St. Paul and Minneapolis, each photograph of a building is indexed

*The Russian-born Copilovich brothers and sisters of St. Paul, about 1918–22. Left to right (standing) are Samuel (Hebrew name Shmuel Behr), Max, Jacob, Henry (who was village president of Hinckley, 1905–8), and (seated) Ida (Mrs. David Gingold), Sam (sometimes known as James, whose Hebrew name was Ishiah and who used the spelling Kopilovich), Sara (Mrs. Max Goldbarg), Gershon (also known as George, and a teacher in a Jewish school), and Molly (Mrs. A. B. Fink). The first to immigrate to Minnesota were Max and Henry; their parents remained in Russia.*

by neighborhood and address. House historians and neighborhood historians find this very useful.

*Access:* Sound and Visual Collections catalog: name of town or county.

**Minnesota Photographers Index**          Sound and Visual Collections

A listing of photographers (from the 1850s to the present) compiled from city directories and business gazetteers. The information includes name(s), address, and years of business. This index is of particular benefit in identifying a time frame for photographs that have a business label.

*Access:* Ask staff for assistance.

**Portraits**          Sound and Visual Collections

Individual portraits, from 1850 to the present. In addition, the portrait catalog also indexes all identified persons who appear prominently in other photographic works in the 250,000-item photo collections. Occasionally, biographical information is attached to the photograph or its availability is noted. Each of the 1,400 formal portraits in the Lee Brothers Historical Photograph Collection has a biographical cover sheet.

*Access:* Sound and Visual Collections: portrait catalog: name of person.

- **PIONEER SETTLERS OBITUARIES AND INDEX**

          Manuscripts Collections

Obituaries of Minnesota pioneer settlers collected by Edwin Clark, 1911–21. The obituaries were clipped from newspapers and pasted in a scrapbook.

*Access:* Manuscripts Collections catalog: Edwin Clark Papers. There is an index with more than 2,000 entries.

- **PLAT BOOKS** *see* Geographical Resources

- **POOR FARM RECORDS**          State Archives

Most Minnesota counties operated poor farms. Some farms date from the 1860s (although most began later in the nineteenth century or early in the twentieth) and continued up to the 1950s. Some became nursing homes or tuberculosis sanatoriums, usually no longer operated by the county. Records of several poor farms are in county records in the State Archives. These usually contain registers of residents (inmates) that give date and cause of application and some or all of the following information: applicant's name, nationality, marital status, age, birthplace, length of residency in state or county, occupation, health status, and death date. *A Historical Directory of Minnesota Homes for the Aged,* by Ethel McClure (St. Paul: Minnesota Historical Society, 1968) may be useful in identifying records of poor farms and municipally owned nursing homes.

*Access:* State Archives notebooks: name of county, Poor Farm.

- **POPULATION RECORDS** *see* Census Records

- **POST OFFICE LOCATION GUIDES** *see* Geographical Resources

- **PRISON RECORDS** *see* Correctional Facilities Records

- **PROBATE RECORDS** *see* Court Records

P

## • PROFESSIONAL CERTIFICATES, LICENSES, AND REGISTRATIONS

Persons desiring to practice various professions or trades in Minnesota have been required to register or to seek a state certificate or license. Licensing and regulatory board records and other materials in the State Archives give personal information about many examinees and licensees. Only some of the occupations are listed here. Published directories of practitioners, or annual or biennial reports of boards and agencies listing licensees are in the Reference Collections; the Manuscripts Collections often contain additional information about persons in medicine, nursing, teaching, and other professions.

**District Court Records**                                          State Archives

Registrations of practitioners of healing in the basic sciences (anatomy, bacteriology, chemistry, hygiene, pathology, and physiology), chiropody (podiatry), chiropractic medicine, dentistry, massage, medicine, the ministry, optometry, osteopathy, and veterinary medicine, as well as notaries public. These practitioners are or have been required to register with the district court in the county in which they are practicing. The registrations may include records of training and other information. District courts also were required to accept credentials of ordinations from individuals licensed to perform marriages in the county.
*Access:* State Archives notebooks: name of county, District Court, Registration and Certificate Records or variant titles.

**Municipal Records**                                              State Archives

Information about peddlers, saloonkeepers, and other persons required to register with or seek licenses from municipal authorities. Such records appear occasionally in municipal records.
*Access:* State Archives notebooks: name of county, municipality.

**Professional Board Records**                                      State Archives

Records include licensing and other information about persons. The information varies according to the record group. Coverage dates, content, indexing, arrangement, and restrictions also vary. The dates given below indicate the earliest and the latest board records in the State Archives, but information about individual licensees may be present for only part of that time. More comprehensive information is in the State Archives notebooks. The boards include:

> Accountancy Board, 1909–70
> Barber Examiners Board, 1897–1980
> Basic Sciences Examiners Board, 1927–74
> Chiropractic Examiners Board, 1919–58
> Cosmetology Board (formerly Board of Hairdressing and Beauty Culture
>     Examiners), 1927–70
> Dental Examiners Board (now Board of Dentistry), 1885–1963
> Electricity Board, 1899–1958
> Law Examiners Board, 1891–1958
> Lawyers Professional Responsibility Board (formerly Board of Professional Responsibility), 1944–87
> Medical Examiners Board (includes records of former Massage Board),
>     1883–1985
> Nursing Board, 1883–1985

Optometry Board, 1899–1984
Osteopathic Examiners and Registration Board, 1903–62
Pharmacy Board, 1885–1975
Watchmakers Board, 1943–83.

*Access:* State Archives notebooks: name of board. Indexes vary for each record group. Access to many records relating to health and legal professions is restricted; examination scores often are protected.

### State Agency Records

P-R

Many state agencies have the authority to register, certify, license, regulate, inspect, or sanction persons and firms in various trades and services. Activities affecting human and animal life and health and finances and property usually are covered. Agency records may contain application or certification information for individual persons. Among such records are those for the following:

*Detective and Protective Agents:* Register (1923–44) in Governor's records and case files (1945–69) in Secretary of State/Corporation Division records, State Archives.

*Embalmers, Morticians, and Funeral Directors:* Lists (1898–1966) in Health Department published records, State Archives.

*Health Care Professionals* (1870s-1980s) in Health Department published records, State Archives.

*Notary Public Appointment and Registration Records*

State Archives

Notaries Public are appointed and commissioned by the governor. Commissions must be recorded with the Administrator of the district court in the county of appointment.

*Access:* State Archives notebooks: name of governor; name of county, District Court, Registrations and Certificates or variant titles; Secretary of State.

Reference Collections

Published lists of Notaries Public are available for various years in the annual and biennial reports of the Secretary of State, 1861–1912, and in *Notaries Public in Minnesota*, 1914–20, published by the office of the Secretary of State.
*Access:* Catalog: Notaries Public — Minnesota.

*Plumbers* (1935–75) in Health Department published records, State Archives.

- **RAILROAD RECORDS** *see also* Land Records

### Published works

Reference Collections

Published materials include histories, timetables, annual reports, and newsletters issued by or about railroad companies and street and electric railways serving Minnesota. For company names, see Richard S. Prosser, *Rails to the North Star* (Minneapolis: Dillon Press, 1966), and Russell L. Olson, *The Electric Railways of Minnesota* (Hopkins, Minn.: Minnesota Transportation Museum, 1976) and its *Supplement* (St. Paul: Minnesota Transportation Museum, 1990).
*Access:* Catalog: name of company.

## Duluth, Missabe and Iron Range Railway Company (DM&IR) Payroll Records
Manuscripts Collections

Payroll records for the DM&IR and its two predecessor companies, the Duluth and Iron Range Railroad Company and the Duluth, Missabe and Northern Railway Company. The payrolls are organized by railroad, division and department, and payroll period. They contain the employee's name; job title; pay rate; compensation, including regular and overtime hours; and deductions. The records are fairly complete from 1884 through 1910. After 1910 there are records through 1970 for each year divisible by 10.

*Access:* Manuscripts Collections catalog: Duluth, Missabe and Iron Range Railway Company, Payroll Records. The payrolls are on microfilm and available through Interlibrary Loan.

## Great Northern Railway Company (GN) Records
Manuscript Collections

Histories, correspondence, financial records, minutes, annual reports, newsletters, personnel files and indexes, and payrolls for the GN. The majority of the personnel files were destroyed before the company records were donated to the MHS. The Society has employee file numbers 1–1587 and 1680–1927; some individual files are missing. A microfilm index (1890s–1900s) in rough alphabetical order gives the employee's name, job title, and employee number; it includes employee numbers 1 to about 383,000. Also on microfilm are annual reports (1880–1968) to GN stockholders. The microfilms are available through Interlibrary Loan.

The GN records include the unindexed business records for more than 250 subsidiary companies. These may contain corporate histories, correspondence, financial records, minutes, annual reports, and payrolls. The payrolls usually give employee name and number, job title, pay rate, and hours worked during the pay period.

*Access:* Great Northern Railway Company notebooks. Access to some records is restricted.

*In 1925 these three brothers, all locomotive engineers for the Great Northern Railway, claimed the United States railroad record for length of combined service—a total of 129 years with the GN. From left to right are Frank (59 years old), William (65), and John (64) Maher.*

**Northern Pacific Railway Company (NP) Records**   Manuscripts Collections

Corporate histories, correspondence, financial records, minutes, annual reports, and payrolls for the NP. The payrolls usually give employee name and number, job title, pay rate, and hours worked during the pay period. Payrolls are by department or branch line and are not complete.

The employee personnel files 1–210,000 (started in 1909) may include employment application, age, nationality, birthplace, residence, medical-examination and accident reports, and records of promotions, leaves of absence, dismissals, resignations, suspensions, retirements, and deaths. The personnel files are arranged by employee number; many are missing. A microfilm index in rough alphabetical order gives employee name, number, and job title; it includes employee numbers 1 to about 303,000. Also on microfilm are annual reports (1870–1968) to NP stockholders. The microfilms are available through Interlibrary Loan.

A related source of information is the unindexed daily record of new employees (4 vols.), listing new employees hired from 1909 through 1967. The register gives name, employee number, and hiring date. Another is the personnel reference file, which is an alphabetical list of selected employees (largely administrative and supervisory) with information about appointments, promotions, and other administrative actions.

The NP records include unindexed business records for more than 200 subsidiary companies. These records may contain corporate histories, correspondence, financial records, minutes, annual reports, and payrolls. The payrolls usually give employee name and number, job title, pay rate, and hours worked during the pay period.

The records also contain unindexed employee newsletters issued by individual departments or the Advertising and Publicity Department.
*Access:* Northern Pacific Railway Company notebooks. Access to some records is restricted.

- **RELIGIOUS RECORDS** *see also* Business Records: Incorporation Records; Newspapers; Oral Histories; Work Projects Administration (WPA) Resources

**General Collections**                                        Manuscripts Collections

Records of Christian churches in Minnesota may include baptisms, marriages, funerals, and other sacraments; lists of members; minutes of congregational or parish meetings and of women's, laymen's, and youth organizations; constitutions and bylaws; financial records; Sunday school records; bulletins; anniversary publications; and reports by, and biographical information about, ministers or priests. Synagogue/temple records contain similar types of information relevant to Jewish religious traditions. While the MHS holds records for many individual churches and religious groups in Minnesota, it has only a minority of those that have existed in the state. Most records remain within their institutions. Some early records may be in languages other than English.
*Access:* Manuscripts Collections catalog: name of town; name of church, synagogue, or temple; denomination; name of priest, minister, or rabbi.

**Church Histories**                                          Reference Collections

General histories of Christian denominations, histories of specific congregations and/or churches, minutes of annual meetings, and church bulletins and periodicals. A general history of Methodism in Minnesota, for example, will focus on the more prominent men and women of that denomination. Jubilee

# R

S. BERNAD.  C. LARSON.  P. WESTLUND.  D. SKOGLUN.  L. M. MAGNUSON.  E LARSON.  E. TIBLING.  F. TILLBERG.  C. JOHNSON.  A. HENRIKSON.  J. ROOSE.
MISS PETERSON.    MISS SVENSON.        C. E. LUNDHOLM.      MISS SVENSON.    MISS OSLUND.    MISS CARLSON.
FÖRSTA SVENSKA BAPTIST-FÖRS. S. S. LÄRARE, NO. I, ST. PAUL, MINN. 1898.

*The first Sunday school teachers of the First Swedish Baptist Church, St. Paul, appear in this 1898 photograph by A. Anderson.*

or anniversary booklets often include such items as membership lists and the names of confirmation-class members and the clergy. Minutes of a denomination's annual meeting may include names of newly ordained ministers, persons licensed to preach, names and residence of current clergy, lists of delegates to the meeting, and biographies of recently deceased clergy. Church bulletins and periodicals may contain information about weekly or monthly activities.
*Access:* Catalog: name of denomination or individual church.

### Episcopal Church Records                          Manuscripts Collections

Documentation of the organization, administration, function, and history of the Protestant Episcopal Church, Diocese of Minnesota, and its parishes, missions (including Minnesota American Indian mission churches), officials, and leaders. The records include parish histories, historical information, financial and organizational records, sermons, lectures, minutes, diaries, clippings, biographical information, scrapbooks, and reports, as well as some parish records.
*Access:* Manuscripts Collections catalog: Protestant Episcopal Church, Diocese of Minnesota. The individual parishes are not listed; researchers should scan the inventory to locate a particular parish. Access to records for the most recent 25 years is restricted.

### Roman Catholic Records                          Manuscripts Collections

Questionnaires sent in 1948 by the Catholic Archdiocese of St. Paul and Minneapolis (Minnesota, North Dakota, and South Dakota) to each of its parishes. The questionnaires gathered information about persons, events, and dates significant in parish history; inventories of parish records; buildings; cemeteries; parish organizations; parochial school programs; and the ethnic composition and geographical origins of parish members. Many parishes sent additional information such as anniversary celebration materials. These materials may be in languages other than English. The questionnaires do *not* include sacramental records (for baptisms, marriages, funerals).

*Access:* Manuscripts Collections catalog: Catholic Archdiocese of St. Paul and Minneapolis. The records are organized alphabetically—by name of state, within each state by name of city, and within each city by name of parish. They are on microfilm and available through Interlibrary Loan.

### United Church of Christ Records                Manuscripts Collections

Records documenting the organization, functions, congregations, and administration of the Minnesota Conference of the United Church of Christ and its predecessor organizations, the Congregational Conference of Minnesota and the Evangelical and Reformed Church, Northern Synod. Included are records of several organizations, such as women's, laymen's, and youth groups; records of geographical subdivisions of the state organization; and the administration records of the Conference. Records of some individual churches are included.

*Access:* Manuscripts Collections catalog: United Church of Christ, Minnesota Conference; Congregational Conference of Minnesota; Evangelical and Reformed Church, Northern Synod. While individual churches do not always have separate entries in the catalog, they are listed in the inventory.

### Work Projects Administration (WPA), Historical Records Survey, Churches
Manuscripts Collections

Information gathered by the WPA in the late 1930s and early 1940s. The church history form includes name, denomination, and location of church; date established; any denominational or name changes; names of present officers; number of original members; number of present members; information about church buildings; names of pastors and dates of service; church cemetery; languages used for services; publications; and official records of church and its organizations. The records are not complete for the entire state.

*Access:* Manuscripts Collections catalog: Work Projects Administration. The records are arranged alphabetically—by name of county, within each county by name of city or township, and then by name of church.

- **RURAL CREDIT DEPARTMENT RECORDS** *see* Land Records

- **SCANDINAVIAN AMERICANS: RESOURCES** *see* Ethnic Resources; Oral Histories; Appendix 1: Ethnic Sources

- **SCHOOL RECORDS**

### College and University Resources

Records of a few colleges and universities held by the State Archives and the Manuscripts Collections may include names of staff and students in various sets of minutes and student enrollment records. The Reference Collections holds items published by a college or university that may include proceedings or minutes of faculty or advisory meetings, yearbooks, student magazines or newspapers, histories of the institution, and alumni lists.

*Access:* State Archives notebooks: name of state university. Manuscripts Collections catalog: name of college or university, or as a subheading under Schools, Minnesota. Access to some records may be restricted. Reference Collections catalog: name of college or university.

Records providing countywide information about teachers and students. Until the office of Superintendent of Schools was abolished by the counties between 1950 and 1971, the Superintendent received or compiled the following types of records containing genealogical information: teachers' annual or term reports, which include lists of pupils with ages, sex, and attendance records; school censuses, with information about school-age children and their families in the county; permanent pupil record cards, with comprehensive information about the student while he or she was in the district; lists of teachers, school officers, and other personnel; teacher examination and certification records; and teachers insurance and retirement fund records. The records occasionally contain poll lists for school elections.

Records are not complete for all counties, and there are none for some counties. Those records in the State Archives, however, usually cover several decades. Some series of records begin in the nineteenth century.

Access: State Archives notebooks: name of county, Superintendent of Schools. Access to some information is restricted.

**S**

*Schoolhouse, District #64, Holst Township, Clearwater County, in 1902. Twenty-four pupils of various ages stand in front of sisters Maude and Grace Jane Baumann, the school's first and second teachers, respectively (left to right in doorway).*

**Private School Records**                    Manuscripts Collections

Records of several private elementary and secondary schools. The records contain names of trustees, faculty and other personnel, alumni, and students in various sets of minutes, programs, directories, and newsletters.

*Access:* Manuscripts Collections catalog: name of school, or as a subheading under Schools, Minnesota. Access to some records is restricted.

**School District Records**                            State Archives

Records of approximately 3,000 rural and independent districts. The records vary greatly in their completeness, both in date spans and in types of records. Some of the school districts still exist today; others were consolidated.

The records include clerk's and treasurer's financial records; school board minutes; pupil records; class records; teacher certification records; student and family censuses; class lists; school officer lists; records of auxiliary organizations, such as parent-teacher associations; records of teacher reading circles and various student clubs; library and textbook records; district consolidation records; records of school elections; and administrative records of several county Superintendents of Schools. Names of students appear in several record types and are found readily in the censuses, class lists, class records, and pupil records. Names of teachers are found in various teacher and student records, as well as in any financial records that contain payrolls. Names of school-board members and officers can be found in the board minutes and financial records.

*Access:* State Archives notebooks: name of county, school district number. Access to certain school records is restricted.

**School Publications** *see also* Newspapers

Reference Collections

Published works from about 35 Minnesota college-level institutions and 250 junior and senior high schools. Publications from colleges (state, private, and community-governed two- and four-year schools) include class bulletins, literary works, yearbooks, and histories. Yearbooks are the basic resource for secondary schools.

*Access:* Catalog: name of school; title of yearbook. Some publications are indexed.

**State Special Education Facilities Records**          State Archives

Records of the Minnesota State Public School in Owatonna (1885–1947) for dependent and neglected children; the Minnesota School for the Deaf (now the Minnesota State Academy for the Deaf), organized in Faribault in 1858; and the Minnesota School for the Blind (now the Minnesota State Academy for the Blind), organized in Faribault in 1863. Records vary from facility to facility, but may include admission and discharge records, students' educational records, and population reports. Administrative records documenting the governance and operation of the facilities include minutes, annual and biennial reports, summary financial records, and operating records. Nonresident records include personnel and payroll records dated before 1940.

*Access:* State Archives notebooks: name of city in which facility is or was located. Access to certain records is restricted.

S

- **SECRETARY OF STATE RECORDS** *see* Business Records: Incorporation Records; Election Records; Motor Vehicle and Driver's License Registration Records; Professional Certificates, Licenses, and Registrations

- **SERVICE ORGANIZATIONS RECORDS** *see* Organizations Records

- **SIOUX INDIANS: RESOURCES** *see* American Indians: Resources

- **SOCIAL ORGANIZATIONS RECORDS** *see* Organizations Records

- **STATE HISTORIC PRESERVATION OFFICE (SHPO) INVENTORY OF HISTORIC PROPERTIES**              State Historic Preservation Office

The SHPO files contain documentation about more than 1,425 listings on the National Register of Historic Places, representing over 4,900 individual properties. The files also contain inventory records with photographs and addresses of nearly 40,000 properties in Minnesota. The files are arranged by county and civil subdivision.

*Access:* By appointment only. For more information, see Appendix 2: Location, Hours, and Telephone Numbers.

- **STATE LAND OFFICE RECORDS** *see* Land Records

- **TAX AND ASSESSMENT RECORDS**              State Archives

Assessment rolls and tax lists for 33 counties. Assessment rolls for real property include the property owner's name and the legal land description, as well as building and land values used to provide estimated market value, and classification and assessed value of each parcel of property. Assessment rolls for personal property include the property owner's name with assessed value for such items as livestock, jewelry, furniture, household and farm items, and other personal holdings. Tax lists include only summary financial information and indicate the actual amount of taxes paid on each person's real and personal property.

The records are usually in the State Archives for the years 1901 and before, and for the years ending in 0 and 1 in the twentieth century through 1961. Assessment rolls and tax lists not in the State Archives may be held by the individual county. Some sets are available only on microfilm.

*Access:* State Archives notebooks: name of county, County Assessor (for assessment rolls) and County Auditor (for tax lists). The records are arranged chronologically, then alphabetically by political subdivision. Some sets are on microform and available through Interlibrary Loan.

- **TEACHERS RETIREMENT ASSOCIATION RECORDS**      State Archives

Teachers Insurance and Retirement Fund records, 1915–31. Included are annual reports submitted by the county Superintendents of Schools to the Teachers Retirement Association listing the name of each teacher, district number, total years teaching experience, number of years in district, number of months in session, number of months taught, annual salary, and retirement deduction. The records also include applications and affidavits for teachers working in publicly funded schools in 1915 and miscellaneous applications. Applications include teachers' work history before 1915.

*Access:* State Archives notebooks: Teachers Retirement Association. There is an incomplete and undated numerical and alphabetical index of teachers belonging to the fund.

- **TOPOGRAPHIC MAPS** *see* Geographical Resources

- **TOWNSHIP RECORDS** *see also* Geographical Resources

State Archives

Records of about 750 townships, many dating from the organization of townships in the 1850s and 1860s. Included are Clerk's and Treasurer's books, Board of Audit minutes, annual meeting minutes, and road record books. Names of township officers and residents and their activities are available in these records. Residents' names also may be found in birth and death registers (ending 1953) maintained by the Township Clerk; burial permits; Justice-of-the-Peace docket books; chattel mortgage record books and indexes; real and personal property assessment books; land, road, and poll tax lists; warrant books; poll lists; and bounty records for wolves, trees, gophers, grasshoppers, and crows. Not all of these records are extant for each township.
*Access:* State Archives notebooks: name of county, county office, township. Access to birth records is restricted.

- **TRADE UNION RECORDS** *see* Union Records

- **UNION RECORDS** Manuscripts Collections

Union membership lists and dues paid and delinquent; lists of members accused of working for nonunion companies; requests for membership information; validations of membership; correspondence; meeting minutes; scrapbooks; election of officers; and information about training programs. Records date from the 1880s through the 1970s.
*Access:* Manuscripts Collections catalog: name of union, name of occupation or profession, name of officer. Access to some records may be restricted by donor.

- **UNITED STATES GENERAL LAND OFFICE RECORDS** *see* Land Records

- **UNITED STATES GOVERNMENT DOCUMENTS**  Reference Collections

As a partial depository for U.S. Government Documents, the MHS selects and holds items that are pertinent to its collections, including the *Serial Set, Congressional Record,* Congressional directories, government employee lists *(Official Record),* publications relating to Indian affairs, geographic names (both national and foreign), post office listings, military officer listings, and census statistics.
*Access:* Reference Collections catalog; *Monthly Catalog of Government Publications,* located in the Reading Room.

- **VETERANS' RECORDS** *see* Military and Veterans' Records

- **VITAL RECORDS** *see also* Township Records; Appendix 3: Vital Records Repositories

The MHS generally does *not* have birth, marriage, or death records, except those that occasionally appear in books, manuscripts, and State Archives records; there is no master index to these materials. Vital records are kept in county courthouses and State Vital Records. For information and years, see Appendix 3: Vital Records Repositories.

An exception to the lack of marriage records held by the MHS is a small file of marriage licenses and certificates of marriage issued in St. Croix County, Wisconsin Territory, 1843–49. These records document marriages occurring west of the St. Croix River in what became Minnesota. The marriages occurred throughout what is now Minnesota and are not limited to the area that is now Washington County.

*Access:* State Archives notebooks: Washington County, District Court, Marriage Records.

- **WARD MAPS** *see* Geographical Resources

- **WOMEN IN INDUSTRY SURVEY**                                    State Archives

Information, compiled by the Minnesota Commission of Public Safety, about firms employing women and about individual female employees in 1918. The information about a firm includes wages, hours, and working conditions. The information about an employee includes name, age, country of birth, nationality, kind of work, wages per week, whether living at home, whether contributing to family support, marital status, whether son or husband is in war service, husband's present employment, husband's wages per week, and ages of children. A separate history sheet for married women with dependents gives employee's name; age; country of birth; marital status; family information, including child care; name of employer; distance of workplace from home; income; and relief needs.

*Access:* State Archives notebooks: Public Safety Commission, Woman's Committee, Survey of Women in Industry. The records are arranged by names of county and employer. They are not indexed.

*In 1904 Josephine Fiorito married a member of the Chickett family in St. Paul. The other identified persons in this photograph by Narsice A. Giguere are Mary Palumbo (far left, standing), Josephine Palumbo (seated), and Kate Garbrarino (center, standing).*

• **WORK PROJECTS ADMINISTRATION (WPA) RESOURCES** *see also* Cemetery Records; Local and County Histories; Religious Records; School Records

Minnesota WPA projects in the late 1930s and early 1940s produced a variety of published histories and manuscript materials, including information about church congregations, school districts, and cemeteries and other background research for county histories, some of which were never completed.

**Annals of Minnesota**  Manuscripts Collections

Microfilmed transcripts of nineteenth-century Minnesota newspaper articles. Subject and geographical headings include Counties, Immigration and Settlement, Names—Persons, and Nationality Groups.
*Access:* Manuscripts Collections catalog: Minnesota Federal Writers' Project, Annals of Minnesota. The transcripts are available through Interlibrary Loan.

**Published Materials**  Reference Collections

Some of the information collected in Minnesota by the Historical Records Survey (HRS) of the WPA was published as *Inventory of the County Archives of Minnesota* (published 1937–42; 44 vols.); *Directory of Churches and Religious Organizations in Minnesota* (published 1942; 583 p.); *Guide to Church Vital Statistics Records in Minnesota: Baptisms, Marriages, Funerals* (published 1942; 253 p.); and *Guide to Public Vital Statistics Records in Minnesota* (published 1941; 142 p.). They describe the records available in county courthouses and individual churches as of about 1943, but do *not* duplicate the records themselves. Not all Minnesota county archives inventories were published. The Reference Collections include many similar HRS publications for other states. Additional printed materials about WPA projects include local history, but rarely mention specific persons.
*Access:* Catalog: Minnesota Historical Records Survey; United States, Work Projects Administration, Minnesota; United States, Works Progress Administration, Minnesota.

**Unpublished Materials**  Manuscripts Collections

Background files for unpublished Minnesota county histories, including interviews with early settlers. Historical information on individual Minnesota churches and cemeteries gathered by WPA workers for possible publication.
*Access:* Manuscripts Collections catalog: Works Progress Administration; Minnesota Federal Writers' Project. The box lists included within the inventories serve as indexes.

# APPENDIX 1

## Selected Sources for Historical and Genealogical Research

Listed below is a selection of general historical and genealogical sources useful to researchers in Minnesota genealogy. Other helpful publications are described in the Genealogical Resources section of this guide in the entries for:

American Indians: Resources
Biographical Records: Biography Reference Sets
Census Records
Family Histories
Geographical Resources: Post Office Location Guides
Military and Veterans' Records: Pension Records Indexes
Passenger Ship Lists
Professional Certificates, Licenses, and Registrations:
    State Agency Records: Notary Public Appointment and Registration
    Records
Work Projects Administration (WPA) Resources: Published Materials.

### MINNESOTA HISTORICAL SOURCES

Andreas, A. T. *An Illustrated Historical Atlas of the State of Minnesota.* Chicago: A. T. Andreas, 1874. Reprint. Evansville, Ind.: Unigraphic, 1976. [324] p. Indexed in *A Comprehensive Index to A. T. Andreas' Illustrated Historical Atlas of Minnesota-1874,* by Mary Hawker Bakeman (Brooklyn Park, Minn.: Park Genealogical Books, 1992).

Blegen, Theodore C. *Minnesota: A History of the State.* 2d ed. Minneapolis: University of Minnesota Press, 1975. 731 p.

*The Book of Minnesotans: A Biographical Dictionary of Leading Living Men of the State of Minnesota,* edited by Albert N. Marquis. Chicago: A. N. Marquis and Company, 1907. 572 p.

Brook, Michael, comp. *Reference Guide to Minnesota History: A Subject Bibliography of Books, Pamphlets, and Articles in English.* St. Paul: Minnesota Historical Society, 1974. 132 p. Followed by *A Supplement to Reference Guide to Minnesota History: A Subject Bibliography, 1970–80,* compiled by Brook and Sarah P. Rubinstein (St. Paul: Minnesota Historical Society Press, 1983; 69 p.).

Clark, Clifford E., Jr., ed. *Minnesota in a Century of Change: The State and Its People Since 1900.* St. Paul: Minnesota Historical Society Press, 1989. 633 p.

Folwell, William Watts. *A History of Minnesota*. Rev. ed. 4 vols. St. Paul: Minnesota Historical Society, 1956–69. The classic account of Minnesota's history from the seventeenth to the early-twentieth centuries.

*Gale Directory of Publications and Broadcast Media: (Formerly Ayer Directory of Publications): An Annual Guide to Publications and Broadcasting Stations*, ed. Karin E. Koek and Julie Winklepleck. 123d ed. 3 vols. Detroit: Gale Research, 1991. Published annually since 1869. For Minnesota publications, see 1:1063–1115.

Gregory, Winifred, ed. *American Newspapers: 1821–1936: A Union List of Files Available in the United States and Canada*. New York: H. W. Wilson Company, 1937. 791 p. For Minnesota newspapers, see p. 321–43.

Hage, George S. *Newspapers on the Minnesota Frontier: 1849–1860*. St. Paul: Minnesota Historical Society, 1967. 176 p.

Harpole, Patricia C., and Mary D. Nagle, eds. *Minnesota Territorial Census, 1850*. St. Paul: Minnesota Historical Society, 1972. 115 p.

Heilbron, Bertha L. *The Thirty-Second State: A Pictorial History of Minnesota*. St. Paul: Minnesota Historical Society, 1966. 306 p.

Holbrook, Franklin F. *Minnesota in the Spanish-American War and the Philippine Insurrection*. St. Paul: Minnesota War Records Commission, 1923. 675 p.

———, and Livia Appel. *Minnesota in the War with Germany*. 2 vols. St. Paul: Minnesota Historical Society, 1928–32. A history of the state's participation in World War I.

Kinney, Gregory, and Lydia Lucas. *A Guide to the Records of Minnesota's Public Lands*. St. Paul: Division of Archives and Manuscripts, Minnesota Historical Society, 1985. 121 p.

Kunz, Virginia Brainard. *Muskets to Missiles: A Military History of Minnesota*. St. Paul: Minnesota Statehood Centennial Commission, 1958. 198 p.

Lass, William E. *Minnesota: A Bicentennial History*. New York: W. W. Norton & Company, 1977. 224 p.

*Little Sketches of Big Folks, Minnesota 1907: An Alphabetical List of Representative Men of Minnesota, with Biographical Sketches*. St. Paul: R. L. Polk, 1907. 441 p.

Meissner, Dennis E. *Guide to the Use of the 1860 Minnesota Population Census Schedules and Index*. St. Paul: Division of Archives and Manuscripts, Minnesota Historical Society, 1978. 21 p.

Minnesota, Secretary of State. *Legislative Manual*. A reference book, on all branches and agencies of state government, that contains some historical material; published biennially by the office of the Secretary of State (St. Paul, 1859–60–   ).

Minnesota Board of Commissioners on Publication of History of Minnesota in Civil and Indian Wars. *Minnesota in the Civil and Indian Wars, 1861–1865*. 2 vols. St. Paul, 1890–93. Volume 1 contains regimental narratives and rosters; volume 2 contains Official Reports and Correspondence. A second edition, embodying some corrections, was published in 1891–99. Indexed in *Minnesota in the Civil and Indian Wars: An Index to the Rosters*, compiled as a

WPA project for the MHS (1936); available in the MHS Reference Collections, the Manuscripts Collections, and the State Archives.

*Minnesota Guidebook to State Agency Services.* St. Paul: Office of the State Register, 1977–   .

Minnesota Historical Society. *Collections.* Articles relating to Minnesota history, published by the MHS, 1872–1920 (vols. 1–17). Available on microfilm. Volume 14 (1912) contains "Minnesota Biographies, 1655–1912," compiled by Warren Upham and Rose B. Dunlap. Indexed in *Collections of the Minnesota Historical Society: Volumes 1–17: Contents and Indexes to the Microfilm Edition* (St. Paul: Minnesota Historical Society, 1980).

––––. *Gopher Historian.* A periodical about Minnesota history for young people, published by the MHS, 1946–72 (succeeded by *Roots*). Indexed in *A Complete Index to the Gopher Historian: 1946–1972* (St. Paul: Minnesota Historical Society Press, 1977). Selected articles published in *Gopher Reader: Minnesota's Story in Words and Pictures – Selections from the Gopher Reader,* edited by A. Hermina Poatgieter and James Taylor Dunn (St. Paul: Minnesota Historical Society and Minnesota Statehood Centennial Commission, 1966; 308 p.), and *Gopher Reader II: Minnesota's Story in Words and Pictures – Selections from the Gopher Historian,* edited by Poatgieter and Dunn (St. Paul: Minnesota Historical Society Press, 1975; 300 p.).

––––. *Minnesota History.* A scholarly journal about Minnesota history published by the MHS since 1915. Volumes 1–5 (1915–24) are entitled *Minnesota History Bulletin.* Indexed in *Minnesota History . . . Index and Classified List of Articles: Volumes I-X* (1915–29; St. Paul: Minnesota Historical Society, 1931), and *Consolidated Index to Minnesota History: Volumes 11–40 (1930–67),* edited by Helen T. Katz (St. Paul: Minnesota Historical Society Press, 1983). A consolidated index for volumes 41–50 (1968–87) is in progress.

––––. *Roots.* A periodical about Minnesota history for young people, published three times a year by the MHS Education Division (succeeding *Gopher Historian*; 1973–   ). Each issue focuses on one topic, such as the Civil War, immigration, folklife, or government.

Patera, Alan H., and John S. Gallagher. *The Post Offices of Minnesota.* Burtonsville, Md.: The Depot, 1978. 280 p. Arranged alphabetically by county, with names of post offices, first postmasters, and dates of operation.

Shutter, Marion D., and J. S. McLain, eds. *Progressive Men of Minnesota: Biographical Sketches and Portraits of the Leaders in Business, Politics and the Professions: Together with an Historical and Descriptive Sketch of the State.* Minneapolis: Minneapolis Journal, 1897. 514 p.

Stuhler, Barbara, and Gretchen Kreuter, eds. *Women of Minnesota: Selected Biographical Essays.* St. Paul: Minnesota Historical Society Press, 1977. 402 p.

Treude, Mai. *Windows to the Past: A Bibliography of Minnesota County Atlases.* Minneapolis: Center for Urban and Regional Affairs, University of Minnesota, 1980. 187 p.

Toensing, W. F. *Minnesota Congressmen, Legislators, and other Elected State Officials: An Alphabetical Check List, 1849–1971.* St. Paul: Minnesota Historical Society, 1971. 143 p.

Upham, Warren. *Minnesota Geographic Names: Their Origin and Historic*

*Significance.* 1920; reprint, St. Paul: Minnesota Historical Society, 1969. 788 p. The standard guide for information about Minnesota place names; first published as volume 17 of the *Collections* of the MHS. The reprint edition has two supplements listing communities incorporated since 1920 and all place names in the state covered by official decisions of the Minnesota and United States geographic boards.

*The Vincent Atlas of Minnesota.* St. Paul: St. Thomas Academy, 1985. 202 p.

White, Bruce M., comp. *The Fur Trade in Minnesota: An Introductory Guide to Manuscript Sources.* St. Paul: Minnesota Historical Society Press, 1977. 61 p.

———, et al., comps. *Minnesota Votes: Election Returns by County for Presidents, Senators, Congressmen, and Governors, 1857–1977.* St. Paul: Minnesota Historical Society, 1977. 234 p.

*Who's Who among Minnesota Women: A History of Woman's Work in Minnesota from Pioneer Days to Date, Told in Biographies, Memorials and Records of Organizations,* compiled by Mary Dillon Foster. N.p.: Privately published, 1924. 380 p.

*Who's Who in Minnesota,* compiled by C. N. Cornwall and edited by Esther Stutheit. Minneapolis: Minnesota Editorial Association, 1941. 1,239 p.

*Who's Who in Minnesota,* edited by Bernice White. Statehood centennial ed. Seattle: Hugh L. White, 1958. 553 p.

*Who's Who in Minnesota,* edited by Bernice White. [Minneapolis]: Hugh L. White, 1964. 403 p.

## GUIDES TO COLLECTIONS OF THE MINNESOTA HISTORICAL SOCIETY AND THE MINNESOTA REGIONAL RESEARCH CENTERS

Fogerty, James E., comp. *Preliminary Guide to the Holdings of the Minnesota Regional Research Centers.* St. Paul: Minnesota Historical Society, 1975. 20 p. Describes manuscripts and oral history interviews in the collections of the regional research centers. Followed by *Manuscripts Collections of the Minnesota Regional Research Centers: Guide Number 2,* compiled by Fogerty (St. Paul: Division of Archives and Manuscripts, Minnesota Historical Society, 1980; 79 p.).

Goff, Lila Johnson, and James E. Fogerty, comps. *The Oral History Collections of the Minnesota Historical Society.* St. Paul: Minnesota Historical Society Press, 1984. 121 p. Describes oral history interviews that are in the collections of the MHS and the regional research centers.

*A Guide to the Central Minnesota Historical Center.* St. Cloud, Minn.: St. Cloud State University, 1992. 27 p.

*Guide to the Collections of the Northeast Minnesota Historical Center.* Duluth, Minn.: The Center, 1988. 68 p.

*Guide to the Northwest Minnesota Historical Center Collections.* Moorhead, Minn.: Livingston Lord Library, Moorhead State University, 1988. 84 p.

*Guide to the West Central Minnesota Historical Center.* Morris: University of Minnesota-Morris; St. Paul: Minnesota Historical Society, 1992. 87 p.

Nute, Grace Lee, and Gertrude W. Ackermann, comps. *Guide to the Personal Papers in the Manuscripts Collections of the Minnesota Historical Society*. St. Paul: Minnesota Historical Society, 1935. 146 p. Followed by *Manuscripts Collections of the Minnesota Historical Society: Guide Number 2*, compiled by Lucile M. Kane and Kathryn A. Johnson (St. Paul: Minnesota Historical Society, 1955; 212 p.), and *Manuscripts Collections of the Minnesota Historical Society: Guide Number 3*, compiled by Lydia A. Lucas (St. Paul: Minnesota Historical Society, 1977; 189 p.).

## GUIDES TO OTHER COLLECTIONS IN NORTH AMERICA

Danky, James P., ed. *Genealogical Research: An Introduction to the Resources of the State Historical Society of Wisconsin*. Madison: State Historical Society of Wisconsin, 1986. 50 p.

*Directory of Archives and Manuscript Repositories in the United States*. 2d ed. Phoenix: Oryx Press, 1988. 853 p. Produced by the National Historical Publications and Records Commission.

*Directory of Historical Organizations in the United States and Canada*, ed. Mary Bray Wheeler. 14th ed. Nashville, Tenn.: AASLH Press, American Association for State and Local History, 1990. 1,108 p.

Goodrum, Charles A., and Helen W. Dalrymple. *Guide to the Library of Congress*. Washington, D.C.: Library of Congress, 1982. 119 p.

Gordon, Robert S., director, and E. Grace Maurice, ed. *Union List of Manuscripts in Canadian Repositories / Catalogue Collectif des Manuscrits des Archives Canadiennes*. Rev. ed. 2 vols. Ottawa: Public Archives of Canada, 1975.

Hinding, Andrea, et al. *Women's History Sources: A Guide to Archives and Manuscript Collections in the United States*. 2 vols. New York: R. R. Bowker, 1979. For collections in Minnesota, see 1:512–89.

Munden, Kenneth W., and Henry Putney Beers. *Guide to Federal Archives Relating to the Civil War*. Washington. D.C.: National Archives and Records Service, General Services Administration, 1962. 721 p.

*The National Union Catalog of Manuscript Collections*. Washington, D.C.: Library of Congress, 1959–   . Published annually. Indexed in *Index to Personal Names in the National Union Catalog of Manuscript Collections* (Alexandria, Va.: Chadwyck-Healey, 1988; 2 vols.).

Szucs, Loretto Dennis, and Sandra Hargreaves Luebking. *The Archives: A Guide to the National Archives Field Branches*. Salt Lake City, Utah: Ancestry Publishing Company, 1988. 340 p.

United States, National Archives and Records Service. *Guide to the National Archives of the United States*. Washington, D.C.: National Archives, 1974. 884 p.

## ETHNIC SOURCES

Researchers seeking information about ethnic groups in Minnesota should first consult *They Chose Minnesota: A Survey of the State's Ethnic Groups*, edited by June Drenning Holmquist (St. Paul: Minnesota Historical Society Press,

1981; 614 p.). This ground-breaking volume contains detailed information about more than sixty ethnic groups who have lived in Minnesota. Other useful sources include:

Anuta, Michael J. *Ships of Our Ancestors.* [Menominee, Mich.: Ships of Our Ancestors, 1983.] 380 p.

Baca, Leo. *Czech Immigration Passenger Lists.* Halletsville, Tex.: Old Homestead Publishing Company, 1983–89. 3 vols.

Foster, Janet, and Julia Sheppard. *British Archives: A Guide to Archive Resources in the United Kingdom.* 2d ed. New York: Stockton Press, 1989. 834 p.

Glazier, Ira A., and P. William Filby, eds. *Germans to America: Lists of Passengers Arriving at U.S. Ports, 1850–1855.* Wilmington, Del.: Scholarly Resources, 1988– . 26 vols.

——, ed., and Michael Tepper, associate ed. *The Famine Immigrants: Lists of Irish Immigrants Arriving at the Port of New York, 1846–1851.* Baltimore: Genealogical Publishing Company, 1983– . 5 vols.

*Guide to Swedish-American Archival and Manuscript Sources in the United States.* Chicago: Swedish-American Historical Society, 1983. 600 p.

Hill, Edward E., comp. *Guide to Records in the National Archives of the United States Relating to American Indians.* Washington, D.C.: National Archives and Records Service, General Services Administration, 1981. 407 p.

Hustvedt, Lloyd, comp. and ed. *Guide to Manuscripts Collections of the Norwegian-American Historical Association.* Northfield, Minn.: The Association, 1979. 158 p.

Koske, Mary T., comp., and Suzanna Moody, ed. *Guide to the Minnesota Finnish American Family History Collection.* [St. Paul]: Immigration History Research Center, University of Minnesota, 1985. 42 p.

Lareau, Paul J., and Elmer Courteau, comps. *French-Canadian Families of the North Central States: A Genealogical Dictionary.* Typescript. St. Paul, 1980. 12 vols., including introductory vol.

Littlefield, Daniel F., Jr., and James W. Parins. *American Indian and Alaska Native Newspapers and Periodicals, 1826–1924.* Westport, Conn.: Greenwood Press, 1984. 482 p.

Minnesota Historical Society. *Chippewa and Dakota Indians: A Subject Catalog of Books, Pamphlets, Periodical Articles, and Manuscripts in the Minnesota Historical Society.* St. Paul: Minnesota Historical Society, 1969. 131 p. A bibliography of printed and manuscript materials about Minnesota's two major American Indian tribes—the Chippewa (or Ojibway) and the Dakota (or Sioux).

*Morton Allan Directory of European Passenger Steamship Arrivals for the Years 1890 to 1930 at the Port of New York and for the Years 1904 to 1926 at the Ports of New York, Philadelphia, Boston and Baltimore.* New York: Immigration Information Bureau, 1931. Reprint. Baltimore: Genealogical Publishing Company, 1979. 268 p.

Newman, Debra L., comp. *Black History: A Guide to Civilian Records in the National Archives.* Washington, D.C.: National Archives Trust Fund Board, General Services Administration, 1984. 379 p.

Olsson, Nils William. *Swedish Passenger Arrivals in New York, 1820–1850.* Chicago: Swedish Pioneer Historical Society, 1967. 391 p.

———. *Swedish Passenger Arrivals in U.S. Ports, 1820–1850 (Except New York): With Additions and Corrections to Swedish Passenger Arrivals in New York, 1820–1850.* St. Paul: North Central Publishing Company, 1979. 139 p.

Rottenberg, Dan. *Finding Our Fathers: A Guidebook to Jewish Genealogy.* New York: Random House, 1977. 401 p.

Saucedo, Ramedo J., comp. *Mexican Americans in Minnesota: An Introduction to Historical Sources.* St. Paul: Minnesota Historical Society, 1977. 26 p. Published in connection with the Mexican-American History Project of the MHS Public Affairs Center.

Schenk, Trudy, et al. *The Wuerttemberg Emigration Index.* Salt Lake City, Utah: Ancestry, Inc., 1986–  . 4 vols.

Spangler, Earl. *The Negro in Minnesota.* Minneapolis: T. S. Denison, 1961. 215 p.

Swierenga, Robert P. *Dutch Immigrants in U.S. Passenger Manifests, 1820–1880: An Alphabetical Listing by Household Heads and Independent Persons.* Wilmington, Del.: Scholarly Resources, 1983. 2 vols.

Taylor, David Vassar, comp. *Blacks in Minnesota: A Preliminary Guide to Historical Sources.* St. Paul: Minnesota Historical Society, 1976. 33 p. Published in connection with the Minnesota Black History Project of the MHS Public Affairs Center.

Thernstrom, Stephan, ed. *Harvard Encyclopedia of American Ethnic Groups.* Cambridge: Harvard University Press, Belknap Press, 1980. 1,076 p.

United States Department of the Interior, Library. *Biographical and Historical Index of American Indians and Persons Involved in Indian Affairs.* Boston: G. K. Hall and Company, 1966. 8 vols.

Wynar, Lubomyr R., and Lois Buttlar. *Guide to Ethnic Museums, Libraries, and Archives in the United States.* Kent, Ohio: Program for the Study of Ethnic Publications, School of Library Science, Kent State University, 1978. 378 p.

———, and Anna T. Wynar. *Encyclopedic Directory of Ethnic Newspapers and Periodicals in the United States.* 2d ed. Littleton, Colo.: Libraries Unlimited, 1976. 248 p.

## RELIGIOUS SOURCES

Bantin, Philip C., with Mark G. Thiel. *Guide to Catholic Indian Mission and School Records in Midwest Repositories.* Milwaukee: Marquette University Libraries, Department of Special Collections and University Archives, 1984. 446 p.

Brackney, William H., and Susan M. Eltscher, comps. *A Guide to Manuscript Collections in the American Baptist Historical Society.* Valley Forge, Pa.: American Baptist Historical Society, 1986. 78 p.

Hage, Anne A., comp. *Church Records in Minnesota: A Guide to Parish Records of Congregational, Evangelical, Reformed, and United Church of Christ Churches, 1851–1981.* Minneapolis: Minnesota Conference, United Church of Christ, 1983. 33 p.

Plaut, W. Gunther. *The Jews in Minnesota: The First Seventy-five Years.* American Jewish Communal Histories 3. New York: American Jewish Historical Society, 1959. 347 p.

Saint John's Abbey (Roman Catholic). *Guide to the Holdings: The Archives, Saint John's Abbey and University.* Collegeville, Minn.: Saint John's Abbey Archives, 1980. 10 p.

Thomas, Evangeline, ed. *Women Religious History Sources: A Guide to Repositories in the United States.* New York: R. R. Bowker, 1983. 329 p.

## GENEALOGICAL SOURCES

Andriot, John L., comp. and ed. *Township Atlas of the United States.* McLean, Va.: Documents Index, 1987. 969 p.

Bentley, Elizabeth Petty. *County Courthouse Book.* Baltimore: Genealogical Publishing Company, 1990. 390 p. For Minnesota courthouses, see p. 182–91.

———. *The Genealogist's Address Book.* Baltimore: Genealogical Publishing Company, 1991. 391 p. For Minnesota addresses, see p. 127–30.

Eakle, Arlene, and Johni Cerny, eds. *The Source: A Guidebook of American Genealogy.* Salt Lake City, Utah: Ancestry Publishing Company, 1984. 786 p.

Everton, George B., Sr., ed. *The Handy Book for Genealogists.* 7th ed., rev. and enlarged. Logan, Utah: Everton Publishers, 1981. 378 p.

Minnesota Genealogical Society (MGS). *Minnesota Genealogist.* Vol. 1 (1970)– ; published quarterly. There are indexes (St. Paul: The Society, 1979–89) to volumes 1–19 (1970–88).

Newman, John J. *American Naturalization Processes and Procedures, 1790–1985.* Indianapolis: Family History Section, Indiana Historical Society, 1985. 43 p.

Pope, Wiley R., comp. and ed. *Minnesota Cemeteries in Print: A Bibliography of Minnesota Published Cemetery Inscriptions and Burials, Etc.* St. Paul: Minnesota Family Trees, 1986. 112 p.

———, comp. *Minnesota Genealogical Index.* Vol 1. St. Paul: Minnesota Family Trees, 1984. An every-name index to a variety of Minnesota-related genealogical, biographical, and historical works.

———, and Sarah Fee. *Minnesota Cemetery Locations.* St. Paul: Minnesota Family Trees, 1988. 221 p.

———, et al. *Tracing Your Ancestors in Minnesota: A Guide to the Sources.* 9 vols. St. Paul: Minnesota Family Trees, 1978–88. Guides to sources for the state and its regions.

United States, National Archives and Records Service. *Guide to Genealogical Research in the National Archives.* Washington, D.C.: National Archives and Records Service, 1982. 304 p.

Warren, Paula Stuart, and Ann H. Peterson, comps. *An Introduction to Minnesota Research Sources.* St. Paul: Minnesota Genealogical Society, 1988. 12 p. A booklet containing information about sources at the Minnesota Genealogical Society and elsewhere in the state.

# APPENDIX 2
## Minnesota Historical Society Information

**LOCATION, HOURS, AND TELEPHONE NUMBERS**

Genealogical resources are available as listed below in the Research Center, the Museum Collections, and the State Historic Preservation Office. Researchers may also enjoy a visit to the exhibits at the History Center; see page 61 for map and hours.

Minnesota History Center
 345 Kellogg Boulevard West
 St. Paul, Minnesota 55102–1906

*Research Center*
Information Desk: (612) 296-2143
Hours: Monday, Tuesday, Wednesday, Friday, Saturday 9:00 A.M. to 5:00
   P.M.
  Thursday 9:00 A.M. to 9:00 P.M.
  Closed Sunday and state holidays

 Weyerhaeuser Reference Room
   General research requests. Books, serials and current newspapers, maps, atlases, photographs, sound and visual collections, oral history tapes, manuscripts collections, Minnesota State Archives.

 Ronald M. Hubbs Microfilm Reading Room
   Censuses, newspapers, Minnesota State Archives microfilms, manuscript microfilms, books and serials on microform

 Copy Center        Telephone requests (612) 297-4709
             Fax requests (612) 297-7436
   Photocopies; photographic, film, and audio reproductions

*Museum Collections*         (612) 296-8071
Three-dimensional artifacts. Visits by appointment only.

*State Historic Preservation Office (SHPO)*  (612) 296-5434
SHPO Inventory of Historic Properties. Visits by appointment only.

## SERVICES

### Reference Service

Reference service is available for all MHS collections. This includes staff assistance in using the catalogs, reference books, and finding aids, and help with specific research subjects. Handouts and orientation classes are available for some subjects as well.

It is helpful for researchers to contact the MHS well ahead of a visit, so that the staff can provide better service and verify completion of any necessary permission forms.

Some research requests can be answered by mail. The staff will determine, within time constraints, how comprehensive replies can be. (There is sometimes a small charge for replies to mail or telephone requests. Please inquire for details.) There are specific instructions regarding newspaper research. Older newspapers are not indexed at this time. To search for a birth or marriage announcement or an obituary, the staff *must* have the following information: the name(s) of person(s), the date of birth/marriage/death (including month, day, and year), and the place where the event occurred (the city or the township and county, if possible, for smaller locations). In order to serve as many patrons as possible, a maximum of three requests per letter will be searched.

### Interlibrary Loan (ILL)

The MHS participates on a limited basis in ILL (the loaning of books and microfilms between libraries). Contact the Research Center for a copy of the current MHS policy regarding ILL. There is usually a transaction charge.

### Photoduplication

The MHS handles all photocopy requests in accordance with the copyright law of the United States (Title 17, U.S. Code), which governs the making of photocopies or other reproductions of copyrighted material. Researchers can request photocopies in person or by mail or telephone. The staff will determine whether or not a resource is too fragile to be copied or is subject to other restrictions.

Researchers can purchase photocopies, prints, and slides of many photographs in the Sound and Visual Collections. Contact the Copy Center for a list of services and prices.

Microfilms of certain newspapers, atlases, periodicals, censuses, manuscript collections, and State Archives records may be available for purchase. Contact the Research Center for directions on purchasing microfilms.

There are charges for all of the above photoduplication services. Estimates are available on request.

**MUSEUM EXHIBITS** (612) 296-6126

Hours: Tuesday, Wednesday, Friday, Saturday 10:00 A.M. to 5:00 P.M.
Thursday 10:00 A.M. to 9:00 P.M.
Sunday 12 noon to 5:00 P.M.
Closed most Mondays and on Thanksgiving, Christmas, and New Year's Day; open Monday holidays 10:00 A.M. to 5:00 P.M.

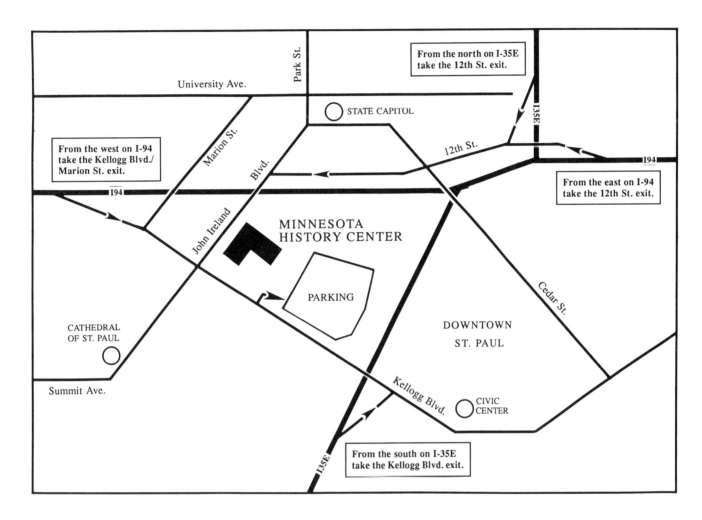

# APPENDIX 3

# General Genealogical Information about Minnesota

The Minnesota Historical Society holds a large number of Minnesota resources, but there are also many other repositories and organizations in the state that have a variety of materials useful to genealogists.

## VITAL RECORDS REPOSITORIES

The MHS does *not* have birth, marriage, or death records, except those that occasionally appear in books, manuscripts, and State Archives records. There is no master index to these materials.

Vital records are kept in the county courthouses. Birth and death records usually begin about 1870 for counties formed by then. Marriage records usually begin about the time of the formation of the county. In 1908 the Minnesota Department of Health began keeping duplicate records of births and deaths.

The best sources for vital information *before* official records were kept are religious records (for baptism, marriage, and death information), census records, death records (birth information is usually included), and obituaries (birth information is sometimes included).

For copies of *official* records, write to the addresses below. A certified copy of a birth record costs $11.00; the cost of a copy of a noncertified birth record is $8.00. A certified copy of a marriage or death record costs $8.00.

| | |
|---|---|
| Minnesota birth and death records, 1908-present | Minnesota Department of Health<br>Section of Vital Statistics Registration<br>717 Delaware Street SE<br>Minneapolis, MN 55440 |
| Minneapolis and Hennepin County birth and death records, 1870-present | Vital Records<br>Hennepin County Government Center<br>300 South Sixth Street<br>Minneapolis, MN 55487 |
| St. Paul birth records, 1867-present; death records, 1870-present; mortuary records, 1866-present | St. Paul Public Health Center<br>555 Cedar Street<br>St. Paul, MN 55101 |

Birth, marriage, and death records for many Minnesota counties—from formation of county to present. For a list of counties, county seats, and zip codes, see below.

Court Administrator
(county name)
Courthouse
(county seat), MN (zip code)

## COUNTY COURTHOUSES

The following list gives the name of each of Minnesota's 87 counties along with the seat—the location of the county courthouse—and the seat's zip code. For information about the formation of the counties, see Upham, *Minnesota Geographic Names* (Appendix 1: Minnesota Historical Sources).

| County | County Seat | Zip Code |
| --- | --- | --- |
| Aitkin | Aitkin | 56431 |
| Anoka | Anoka | 55303 |
| Becker | Detroit Lakes | 56501 |
| Beltrami | Bemidji | 56601 |
| Benton | Foley | 56329 |
| Big Stone | Ortonville | 56278 |
| Blue Earth | Mankato | 56001 |
| Brown | New Ulm | 56073 |
| Carlton | Carlton | 55718 |
| Carver | Chaska | 55318 |
| Cass | Walker | 56484 |
| Chippewa | Montevideo | 56265 |
| Chisago | Center City | 55012 |
| Clay | Moorhead | 56560 |
| Clearwater | Bagley | 56621 |
| Cook | Grand Marais | 55604 |
| Cottonwood | Windom | 56101 |
| Crow Wing | Brainerd | 56401 |
| Dakota | Hastings | 55033 |
| Dodge | Mantorville | 55955 |
| Douglas | Alexandria | 56308 |
| Faribault | Blue Earth | 56013 |
| Fillmore | Preston | 55965 |
| Freeborn | Albert Lea | 56007 |
| Goodhue | Red Wing | 55066 |
| Grant | Elbow Lake | 56531 |
| Hennepin | Minneapolis | * |
| Houston | Caledonia | 55921 |
| Hubbard | Park Rapids | 56470 |
| Isanti | Cambridge | 55008 |
| Itasca | Grand Rapids | 55744 |
| Jackson | Jackson | 56143 |
| Kanabec | Mora | 55051 |
| Kandiyohi | Willmar | 56201 |
| Kittson | Hallock | 56728 |
| Koochiching | International Falls | 56649 |
| Lac qui Parle | Madison | 56256 |
| Lake | Two Harbors | 55616 |

| | | |
|---|---|---|
| Lake of the Woods | Baudette | 56623 |
| Le Sueur | Le Center | 56057 |
| Lincoln | Ivanhoe | 56142 |
| Lyon | Marshall | 56258 |
| McLeod | Glencoe | 55336 |
| Mahnomen | Mahnomen | 56557 |
| Marshall | Warren | 56762 |
| Martin | Fairmont | 56031 |
| Meeker | Litchfield | 55355 |
| Mille Lacs | Milaca | 56353 |
| Morrison | Little Falls | 56345 |
| Mower | Austin | 55912 |
| Murray | Slayton | 56172 |
| Nicollet | St. Peter | 56082 |
| Nobles | Worthington | 56187 |
| Norman | Ada | 56510 |
| Olmsted | Rochester | 55901 |
| Otter Tail | Fergus Falls | 56537 |
| Pennington | Thief River Falls | 56701 |
| Pine | Pine City | 55063 |
| Pipestone | Pipestone | 56164 |
| Polk | Crookston | 56716 |
| Pope | Glenwood | 56334 |
| Ramsey | St. Paul *(county seat and state capital)* | 55102** |
| Red Lake | Red Lake Falls | 56750 |
| Redwood | Redwood Falls | 56283 |
| Renville | Olivia | 56277 |
| Rice | Faribault | 55021 |
| Rock | Luverne | 56156 |
| Roseau | Roseau | 56751 |
| St. Louis | Duluth | 55802 |
| Scott | Shakopee | 55379 |
| Sherburne | Elk River | 55330 |
| Sibley | Gaylord | 55334 |
| Stearns | St. Cloud | 56301 |
| Steele | Owatonna | 55060 |
| Stevens | Morris | 56267 |
| Swift | Benson | 56215 |
| Todd | Long Prairie | 56347 |
| Traverse | Wheaton | 56296 |
| Wabasha | Wabasha | 55981 |
| Wadena | Wadena | 56482 |
| Waseca | Waseca | 56093 |
| Washington | Stillwater | 55082 |
| Watonwan | St. James | 56081 |
| Wilkin | Breckenridge | 56520 |
| Winona | Winona | 55987 |
| Wright | Buffalo | 55313 |
| Yellow Medicine | Granite Falls | 56241 |

*For Minneapolis and Hennepin County birth and death records, write to the Hennepin County Government Center (see Vital Records Repositories, above).

**For St. Paul birth, death, and mortuary records, write to the St. Paul Public Health Center (see Vital Records Repositories). For other Ramsey County vital records, write to the Ramsey County Courthouse.

## HISTORICAL AND GENEALOGICAL ORGANIZATIONS

For information about the state's county historical societies and their chapters, local and regional historical preservation and genealogical organizations, and related museum organizations, contact the MHS Research Center (see Appendix 2 for address and telephone number), or contact:

Field Programs
Minnesota Historical Society
Minnesota History Center
345 Kellogg Boulevard West
St. Paul, MN 55102-1906
(612) 296-5434

### Minnesota Regional Research Centers

The centers were formerly part of a network established by the MHS in the 1960s and 1970s to collect and preserve documentary sources for areas in the state other than Minneapolis and St. Paul. Many of the manuscript collections and oral history interviews at the centers are owned by the Society, but administered by the various institutions that house them. For published guides that describe the collections, see Appendix 1.

The collections at the centers generally do *not* include extensive county or municipal records. For information about these materials, researchers should contact the MHS Research Center.

Contact the regional research centers directly with *specific* requests regarding their collections. Not all of the centers have full-time staffs, so researchers should telephone or write before visiting.

Central Minnesota Historical Center
Centennial Hall, Room 148
St. Cloud State University
St. Cloud, MN 56301
(612) 255-3254

Collections for Aitkin, Benton, Chisago, Crow Wing, Isanti, Kanabec, Mille Lacs, Morrison, Pine, Sherburne, Stearns, Todd, Wadena, and Wright counties

North Central Minnesota Historical Center
The A. C. Clark Library
Bemidji State University
Bemidji, MN 56601
(218) 755-3349 or (218) 755-2955

Collections for Beltrami, Cass, Clearwater, Hubbard, Itasca, Koochiching, and Lake of the Woods counties

Northeast Minnesota Historical Center
University of Minnesota-Duluth
Library 375
Duluth, MN 55812
(218) 726-8526
Collections for Carlton, Cook, Lake, and St. Louis counties

Northwest Minnesota Historical Center
Livingston Lord Library
Moorhead State University
Moorhead, MN 56560
(218) 236-2346
Collections for Becker, Clay, Kittson, Mahnomen, Marshall, Norman, Otter Tail, Pennington, Polk, Red Lake, Roseau, and Wilkin counties

Southern Minnesota Historical Center
Mankato State University
Mankato, MN 56001
(507) 389-1029 or (507) 389-6201
Collections for Blue Earth, Brown, Faribault, Freeborn, Le Sueur, Martin, Nicollet, Rice, Sibley, Steele, Waseca, and Watonwan counties

Southwest Minnesota Historical Center
Southwest State University
BA 509
Marshall, MN 56258
(507) 537-7373 or (507) 537-6294 (History Department)
Collections for Cottonwood, Jackson, Kandiyohi, Lac qui Parle, Lincoln, Lyon, McLeod, Meeker, Murray, Nobles, Pipestone, Redwood, Renville, Rock, and Yellow Medicine counties

West Central Minnesota Historical Center
University of Minnesota-Morris
Morris, MN 56267
(612) 589-2211, extension 6170
Collections for Big Stone, Chippewa, Douglas, Grant, Pope, Stevens, Swift, and Traverse counties

Some of the collections of the former Southeast Minnesota Historical Center at Winona State University (for Dodge, Fillmore, Goodhue, Houston, Mower, Olmsted, Wabasha, and Winona counties) are now housed at the MHS Research Center.

### Iron Range Research Center (IRRC)
The IRRC collection of manuscripts, oral histories, and photographs focuses on the communities of the iron ranges that stretch for about two hundred miles across northeastern Minnesota. The center is also an officially designated, government-records repository for iron-range communities and has a reference library with a full-time library and archives staff. It is located at Ironworld USA (the Iron Range Interpretative Center), which features the mining history and ethnic heritage of the area. Researchers who wish to visit *only* the IRRC should tell this to the staff at the entrance to Ironworld. There is an admission charge for Ironworld, but no charge for the IRRC.

Iron Range Research Center
Highway 169 West
Chisholm, MN
(218) 254-5733
*Mailing address:* P.O. Box 392
Chisholm, MN 55719

### Immigration History Research Center (IHRC)

The IHRC, part of the University of Minnesota, focuses on research materials about immigrants to the United States from Central and Southern European, Eastern, and Near Eastern countries, including such ethnic groups as Czechs, Finns, Greeks, Hungarians, Italians, Latvians, Slovaks, and Ukrainians. While the center has some Minnesota materials, its scope is nationwide.

Immigration History Research Center
826 Berry Street
University of Minnesota
St. Paul, MN 55114
(612) 627-4208

### Minnesota Genealogical Society (MGS)

The MGS (founded in 1969) is an all-volunteer, nonprofit, educational organization for persons interested in genealogical research. There are also branches and groups of the society with special interests, such as ethnic research. The MGS library and classes are open to nonmembers. For more information, contact the MGS or see *Introduction to Minnesota Research Sources*, compiled by Warren and Peterson (Appendix 1: Genealogical Sources).

Minnesota Genealogical Society
Office and Library: 1650 Carroll Avenue
St. Paul, MN
(612) 645-3671

*Mailing address:* P.O. Box 16069
St. Paul, MN 55116-0069

### Church of Jesus Christ of Latter-Day Saints (Mormon) Family History Centers

The following regional church centers have family history research facilities and are open to the general public.

Family History Center
2801 North Douglas Drive
Crystal, MN
(612) 544-2479
*Mailing address:* P.O. Box 27283
Minneapolis, MN 55427

Family History Center
2140 North Hadley
Oakdale, MN 55119
(612) 770-3213

# MINNESOTA COUNTIES AND COUNTY SEATS